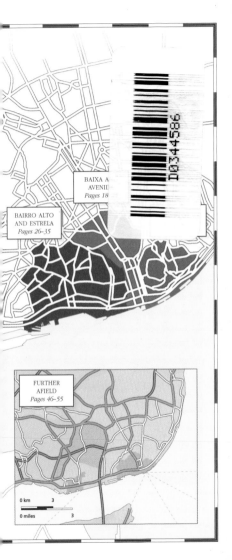

0 km   3

0 miles   3

LONDON, NEW YORK,
MELBOURNE, MUNICH AND DELHI
www.dk.com

Concept created by Redback Publishing
www.redbackpublishing.com

PACKAGED BY
HourGlass Media
www.hourglassmedia.co.uk

REPRODUCED BY
Colourscan (Singapore)

PRINTED AND BOUND
in China by Leo Paper Products Ltd.

First published in Great Britain in 2010
by Dorling Kindersley Limited, 80 Strand, London WC2R 0RL

A CIP CATALOGUE RECORD IS AVAILABLE FROM THE BRITISH LIBRARY.

ISBN 978-1-4053-4688-7

MIX
Paper from
responsible sources
FSC™ C018179
www.fsc.org

**The information in this
DK Eyewitness Travel Guide is checked regularly.**
Every effort has been made to ensure that this book is as up-to-date as
possible at the time of going to press. Some details, however, such
as telephone numbers, opening hours, prices, gallery hanging
arrangements and travel information, are liable to change. The
publishers cannot accept responsibility for any consequences arising
from the use of this book, nor for any material on third-party websites,
and cannot guarantee that any website address in this book will be a
suitable source of travel information. We value the views and
suggestions of our readers highly. Please write to:
Publisher, DK Eyewitness Travel Guides,
Dorling Kindersley, 80 Strand, London WC2R 0RL.

Teatro Nacional Dona Maria II in the Baixa (lower town) area of Lisbon

CONTENTS

Portugal's coat of arms

Sandy beach and promenade along the bay of Estoril

Central Lisbon

Lisbon, the capital of Portugal, is a vibrant and historic city that lies on steep hills on the north bank of the River Tagus. It is an attractive place to explore and walking is one of the best ways to see it. This book divides Lisbon into four easily managed areas, while two further sections look at the major sights that lie beyond the city.

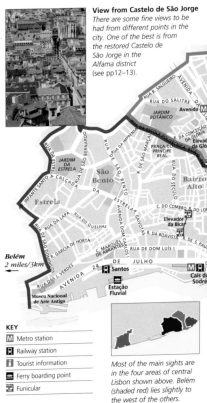

View from Castelo de São Jorge
There are some fine views to be had from different points in the city. One of the best is from the restored Castelo de São Jorge in the Alfama district (see pp12–13).

Belém
2 miles/3km

KEY

M	Metro station
🚆	Railway station
ℹ	Tourist information
⛴	Ferry boarding point
🚡	Funicular

Most of the main sights are in the four areas of central Lisbon shown above. Belém (lies shaded red) slightly to the west of the others.

Torre de Belém
This Statue of Our Lady of Safe Homecoming faces the sea from the defensive Torre de Belém – one of Lisbon's emblems (see p43).

Igreja do Carmo
The Gothic ruins of this 14th-century church are an evocative reminder of the 1755 earthquake (see p28).

0 metres 500
0 yards 500

Triumphal Arch
Leading into Rua Augusta from the Praça do Comércio, this impressive arch is the gateway to Baixa (see pp24–5).

Lisbon's Highlights

On 1 November 1755, a massive earthquake laid waste to central Lisbon. Despite the scale of the devastation, the city was quickly rebuilt. Today, it is filled with inspiring architecture and enchanting squares, and has a lively modern side as well.

The riverside garden at the Museu Nacional de Arte Antiga

Museums and Galleries

Museu Nacional de Arte Antiga
Housed in a 17th-century palace, Portugal's national gallery is a treasure trove of historically illuminating art. Once associated with a certain fustiness, it has recently been sweeping out the cobwebs (see pp32–3).

Museu Nacional do Azulejo
This museum, dedicated to tiles, is enjoyable for the excellent displays and for its beautiful setting – a 16th-century convent transformed over the centuries to include some of the city's prettiest cloisters and one of its most richly decorated churches (see p52).

Museu do Chiado
Located in a stylishly restored warehouse, this museum is dedicated to Portuguese art from the mid-19th century onwards. The core collection dates from 1850–1950, but temporary shows are held for new artists (see p30).

Museu Calouste Gulbenkian
Thanks to Calouste Gulbenkian, a wealthy Armenian oil magnate with wide-ranging tastes and an eye for a masterpiece, this museum has one of the finest collections of art in Europe (see pp50–51).

Churches and Monasteries

Sé
Lisbon's cathedral was built for the city's first bishop in the middle of the 12th century. It is a fortress-like structure that glows amber as the sun sets (see p15).

São Roque
São Roque's plain façade belies a remarkably rich interior. The church was founded at the end of the 16th century for the Jesuit order (see p28).

Mosteiro dos Jéronimos
This magnificent monastery is the culmination of ornate Manueline architecture – a style named after Manual I who commissioned the building (see pp40–41).

One of the many famous tombs inside Mosteiro dos Jéronimos

Igreja de São Domingos

Dark and cavernous, the São Domingos church is not on the tourist trail, despite its long history. As a result, it is a good place for quiet reflection, whatever one's creed (see p21).

Secular Architecture

Torre de Belém

This perfectly proportioned defensive tower at Belém is a jewel of the 16th-century Manueline architectural style, combining Moorish, Renaissance and Gothic elements in a dazzling whole (see p43).

Torre de Belém, one of the city's most recognized landmarks

Castelo de São Jorge

This hilltop castle is thought to be the place where Lisbon's original settlers lived. After centuries of neglect, the castle was imaginatively restored in 1938, providing Lisbon with one of its most attractive viewpoints (see pp12–13).

Casa dos Bicos

Built as a private palace in 1523, this building has an easily identifiable Italianate façade with unusual diamond-shaped stones (bicos). The top floors, ruined in the huge earthquake of 1755, have been restored (see p15).

Palácio Nacional da Ajuda

This Neo-Classical palace in Ajuda is a prime example of regal excess, with its ostentatious rooms and lavish decorations (see p45).

City Views

Miradouro de Santa Luzia

The view from this terrace spans the tiled roofs of the Alfama toward the Tagus. This is a pleasant place to rest after a walk around the area's steep streets (see p10).

Miradouro da Graça

Another splendid viewpoint from which to see Castelo de São Jorge and central Lisbon. The open-air café is a popular meeting point especially in the late afternoons and light summer evenings (see pp16–17).

Miradouro de São Pedro de Alcântara

This belvedere (*miradouro*) commands a sweeping view of eastern Lisbon, seen across the Baixa. A tiled map, placed against the balustrade, helps you locate the landmarks in the city below (see p31).

View from Miradouro de São Pedro de Alcântara

Elevador de Santa Justa

The best close-up overview of the Baixa and Rossio, with the castle above, is to be had from the terrace at the top of the Elevador de Santa Justa (see p23).

ALFAMA

This was once the most desirable quarter of Lisbon, but in the Middle Ages wealthy residents moved west for fear of earthquakes, leaving the quarter to fishermen and paupers. Today, compact houses line steep streets and stairways, and daily life revolves around local stores and small tavernas. Above the Alfama, the imposing Castelo de São Jorge crowns Lisbon's eastern hill.

SIGHTS AT A GLANCE

SEE ALSO

• *Street Life p17*

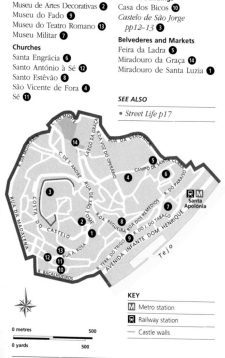

KEY

M	Metro station
R	Railway station
—	Castle walls

0 metres 500
0 yards 500

◀ Houses in the Alfama quarter with the Santa Engrácia dome behind

Tile panel showing pre-earthquake Praça do Comércio, Santa Luzia

Miradouro de Santa Luzia

Map J5. Rua do Limoeiro.

The terrace by the church of Santa Luzia provides a sweeping view over the Alfama and the River Tagus. Distinctive landmarks, from left to right, are the cupola of Santa Engrácia, the church of Santo Estêvão and the two startling white towers of São Miguel. The south wall of Santa Luzia has two modern tiled panels, one of Praça do Comércio before it was flattened by the earthquake, the other showing the Christians attacking the Castelo de São Jorge *(see pp12–13)* in 1147.

Museu de Artes Decorativas ❷

Map J5. Largo das Portas do Sol 2. Open Wed–Mon. Adm charge.

Also known as the Ricardo do Espírito Santo Silva Foundation, the museum was set up in 1953 to preserve the traditions and increase public awareness of the Portuguese decorative arts. The foundation was named after a banker who bought the 17th-century Palácio Azurara in 1947 to house his fine collection of furniture, textiles, silver and ceramics. Among the 17th- and 18th-century antiques on display are many fine pieces in exotic woods, 18th-century silver and Chinese porcelain, and Arraiolos carpets. The spacious rooms still retain some original ceilings and tiled panels. In the workshops next door, artisans preserve the techniques of gilding, cabinet-making, book-binding and other traditional crafts. Temporary exhibitions, lectures and concerts are also held here.

The 17th-century Palácio Azurara, dedicated to the decorative arts

Castelo de São Jorge ❸

See pp12-13.

São Vicente de Fora ❹

Map J4. Largo de São Vicente. Closed for repairs. **Monastery** Open Tue–Sun. Adm charge to cloisters.

Stalls at the Feira da Ladra

St Vincent was proclaimed Lisbon's patron saint in 1173, when his relics were transferred from the Algarve, in southern Portugal, to a church on this site outside (*fora*) the city walls. Designed by Italian architect Filippo Terzi and completed in 1627, the off-white façade is sober and symmetrical. Towers stand on either side of the façade, with statues of saints Augustine, Sebastian and Vincent over the entrance. Inside is Machado de Castro's Baroque canopy over the altar, flanked by life-size wooden statues.

The adjoining former Augustinian monastery retains its 16th-century cistern and vestiges of the former cloister, but is visited for its 18th-century tiles (*azulejos*). Among the panels in the entrance hall, there are lively tile scenes of Afonso Henriques attacking the Portuguese cities of Lisbon and Santarém.

The stone sarcophagi of almost every king and queen are here, from João IV, who died in 1656, to Manuel II, last king of Portugal. Only Maria I and Pedro IV are not buried here. A stone mourner kneels at the tomb of Carlos I and his son Luís Felipe, assassinated in Praça do Comércio in 1908.

Feira da Ladra ❺

Map J4. Campo de Santa Clara. Open Tue & Sat.

This flea market has occupied this site for over a century. As its fame has grown, bargains have become hard to find, but a few of the vendors have interesting wrought-iron work, prints and tiles, as well as second-hand clothes. Evidence of Portugal's colonial past is reflected in the stalls selling African statuary, masks and jewellery. Fish, vegetables and herbs are sold in the central marketplace.

Santa Engrácia ❻

Map J4. Campo de Santa Clara. Open Tue–Sun. Adm charge.

The soaring dome of Santa Engrácia is one of Lisbon's most striking landmarks. The original church was destroyed by a storm in 1681, and although the first stone of the new church was laid in 1682, the church wasn't completed until 1966.

The interior is paved with marble and a lift up to the dome offers a 360-degree panorama of the city. As the National Pantheon, the Santa Engrácia houses monuments to Portugal's most famous personalities, such as the explorer Vasco da Gama.

Castelo de São Jorge ❸

Following the recapture of Lisbon from the Moors in 1147, King Afonso Henriques transformed their hilltop citadel into a royal residence. After the 1755 earthquake, the ramparts remained in ruins until 1938, when it was completely renovated. The castle may not be authentic, but it is a pleasant place for a stroll and boasts fine views of Lisbon.

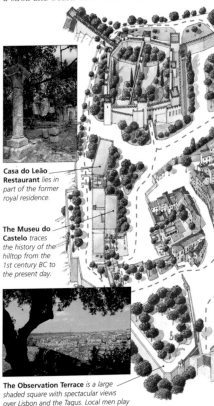

Casa do Leão Restaurant lies in part of the former royal residence.

The Museu do Castelo traces the history of the hilltop from the 1st century BC to the present day.

The Observation Terrace is a large shaded square with spectacular views over Lisbon and the Tagus. Local men play backgammon and cards under the trees.

The ramparts and towers can be walked around. Stop off at the Torre de Ulisses and watch views of Lisbon being projected onto the inside walls.

Porta de Santo André

Santa Cruz is a small quarter made up of narrow streets tightly packed within the walls of the old castle.

Rua de Santa Cruz do Castelo is one of the pretty streets south of the Castelo de São Jorge.

Porta de Saõ Jorge

VISITORS' CHECKLIST

Map H4. Porta de São Jorge, Rua de Santa Cruz do Castelo. Tel 218 800 620. Open daily (times vary). Adm charge. **Torre de Ulisses** Open daily Apr–Sep. Shows every half an hour. **Museum** Open daily.

The imposing façade of the Museu Militar – Lisbon's military museum

Museu Militar ⑦

Map J4–J5. Largo do Museu de Artilharia. Open Tue–Sun (times vary).

Located on the site of a former 16th-century cannon foundry and arms depot, the military museum contains an extensive collection. Visits begin in the Vasco da Gama Room with a collection of old cannons and modern murals depicting the discovery of the sea route to India. The Salas da Grande Guerra contains artefacts related to World War I. Other rooms focus on the evolution of Portuguese weapons, and the large courtyard tells the story of Portugal in tiled panels, from the Christian Reconquest to World War I. The Portuguese artillery section, in the oldest part of the museum, displays the wagon used to transport the triumphal arch to Rua Augusta *(see p23)*.

Santo Estêvão ⑧

Map J5.

The small esplanade in front of the Santo Estêvão church is one of the Alfama area's best viewing points. Access is easy, if steep, from Largo do Chafariz do Dentro, at the foot of Alfama, where you will find one of the city's oldest public fountains (as well as the Fado Museum, so you can easily combine a visit to both). Just head up Rua dos Remédios until you see steps on your left called Escadas de Santo Estêvão; climb them and you're there.

Museu do Fado ⑨

Map J5. Largo do Chafariz de Dentro 1. Open Tue–Sun. Adm charge.

Also called the Casa do Fado e da Guitarra Portuguesa, this museum is dedicated to Lisbon's most famous musical genre known as Fado and to the mandolin-shaped Portuguese "guitar". This instrument, whose strings are arranged in pairs, combines with the singer's soaring tremolos to give Fado – often compared with the Blues – its unique sound. The museum was built recently, only opening in 1998, but its life-size replica of a Fado venue – complete with models of singer, musicians, staff and customers – has an old-fashioned feeling to it. Apart from the exhibits, there is an outdoor café, a store and an auditorium where Fado concerts are often held.

Casa dos Bicos ⑩

Map H5. Rua dos Bacalhoeiros. Not open to the public.

This unusual-looking house, faced with diamond-shaped stones (bicos), was built in 1523 for Brás de Albuquerque, the illegitimate son of Afonso, Viceroy of India. The façade is an adaptation of a style that was popular in 16th-century Europe. The two top storeys, ruined in the massive earthquake of 1755, were restored in the 1980s, recreating the original from old views of Lisbon found in tile panels and engravings. In the interim, the building was used for salting fish (Rua dos Bacalhoeiros means "street of the cod fishermen").

The façade of the city's cathedral, with its castellated bell towers

The curiously faceted Casa dos Bicos and surrounding buildings

Sé ⑪

Map H5. Largo da Sé. Open daily. Adm charge to Gothic cloister and treasury.

In 1150, Afonso Henriques built a cathedral for the first bishop of Lisbon on the site of an old mosque. Sé is short for Sedes Episcopalis, the seat (or see) of a bishop. Following damage by several earthquakes in the 14th century, as well as the one in 1755, the cathedral has been rebuilt over the centuries and comprises a variety of architectural styles. The façade, with its twin bell towers and splendid rose window, retains its solid Romanesque aspect, while its gloomy interior is simple and austere. The ambulatory has nine Gothic chapels and there is also a Gothic cloister. This has elegant double arches with some finely carved capitals. To the left of the cathedral entrance, the Franciscan chapel contains the font where St Vincent was baptized in 1195. The adjacent chapel contains a Baroque nativity scene by Machado de Castro (1766). The treasury houses silver, ecclesiastical robes, statuary, manuscripts and a few relics associated with St Vincent.

Tiled panel recording Pope John Paul II's visit to Santo António à Sé

Santo António à Sé ⑫

Map H5. Largo Santo António à Sé 24. Open daily. **Museu Antoniano** Open Tue–Sun. Adm charge.

This popular little church allegedly stands on the site of the house in which St Antony was born. The crypt is all that remains of the original church that was destroyed in the earthquake of 1755. Work began on the new church in 1757 and was partly funded by donations collected by children with the cry "a small coin for St Antony". Even today, the floor of the chapel in the crypt is strewn with money and the walls are scrawled with messages. Inside, on the way down to the crypt, a tiled panel commemorates the visit of Pope John Paul II in 1982. In 1995 the church was given a facelift for the saint's eighth centenary.

It is traditional for young couples to visit the church of Santo António à Sé on their wedding day and leave flowers for St Antony, who is believed to bring good luck to new marriages.

Next door, the small Museu Antoniano houses artefacts relating to St Antony, plus gold and silverware, which used to decorate the church.

Museu do Teatro Romano ⑬

Map H5. Pátio do Aljube 5. Open Tue–Sun.

A Roman amphitheatre from the 1st century BC lurks beneath the buildings just above the Sé. Not a lot has been excavated yet, but it seems to have been a large structure, seating maybe 5,000. Excavations continue, so visitors can get an insight into archaeological work.

Miradouro da Graça ⑭

Map H4.

The working-class quarter of Graça developed at the end of the 19th century. Today, it is visited chiefly for the views from its belvedere (*miradouro*). The panorama of rooftops and skyscrapers is less spectacular than the view from the castle, but it is a popular spot, particularly in the early evenings when couples sit at café tables under the pines. Behind the *miradouro* stands an Augustinian monastery, founded in 1271 and rebuilt after the earthquake. Once a flourishing complex, the

The Miradouro and Igreja da Graça seen from the Castelo de São Jorge

huge building is nowadays used as a barracks, but the Igreja da Graça church can still be visited. Inside, is the *Senhor dos Passos*, a representation of Christ carrying the cross on the way to Calvary. This figure, clad in purple clothes, is carried on a procession through Graça on the second Sunday in Lent.

STREET LIFE

RESTAURANTS	CAFÉS AND BARS

RESTAURANTS

Hua-Ta-Li
Map H5. Rua dos Bacalhoeiros 109–115. Tel 218 879 170.
Cheap
Large, popular Chinese restaurant close to the docks.

Santo António de Alfama
Map J5. Beco de São Miguel 7. Tel 218 871 487.
Moderate
Good quality modern food and a large choice of dishes.

Lautasco
Map J5. Beco do Azinhal 7a (off Rua de São Pedro). Tel 218 860 173.
Moderate
Rustic restaurant serving typical Portuguese cuisine with outside terrace.

Viagem de Sabores
Map H5. Rua de São João da Praça 103. Tel 218 870 189.
Expensive
This charming restaurant's "tastes journey" gives a great selection of world dishes.

Casa do Leão
Map H4. Castelo de São Jorge. Tel 218 875 962.
Expensive
Grand restaurant with an ambitious Portuguese menu housed in the remains of the Alcáçovas castle. Great views.

See p80 for price codes.

CAFÉS AND BARS

Cerca Moura
Map J5. Largo das Portas do Sol 4.
Popular, largely outdoor bar and café with cosy interior in what was once Moorish Lisbon's town walls.

Cefalópode
Map H4. Largo do Contador-Mor 4B.
Laid-back bar with live music at weekends and jam sessions, poetry readings and art exhibitions on other days.

Ondajazz Bar
Map H5. Arco de Jesus 7.
French-run bar that lays on live jazz and other cool musical choices in this vaulted former coffee warehouse.

Esplanada da Igreja da Graça
Map J4. Largo da Graça.
One of Lisbon's best café-table views is to be had from this esplanade. Particularly good on sunny late afternoons.

Deli Delux
Map J4. Avenida Infante Dom Henrique/Cais da Pedra.
Well-stocked deli with a café serving great brunches.

Chapitô
Map H4. Costa do Castelo 7.
Large friendly bar, café and restaurant with superb views.

BAIXA AND AVENIDA

Following the earthquake of 1755, Lisbon's city centre was completely rebuilt. Based on a grid system, the streets were flanked by uniform, Neo-Classical buildings. The Baixa (lower town) is still the commercial hub of the capital, housing banks, offices and shops. At its centre, Rossio is a popular meeting point with cafés, theatres and restaurants. The streets are crowded by day, but at night the quarter is almost deserted.

SIGHTS AT A GLANCE

Museums and Galleries
Museu da Sociedade de Geografia ❸
Núcleo Arqueológico da Rua dos Correeiros ⓫

Churches
Igreja de São Domingos ❻
Nossa Senhora da Conceição Velha ⓬

Parks and Gardens
Jardim Botânico ❶

Lifts
Elevador de Santa Justa ❾

Historic Streets and Squares
Avenida da Liberdade ❷
Praça da Figueira ❽
Praça do Comércio ⓭
Praça dos Restauradores ❹
Rossio ❼
Rua Augusta ❿
Rua das Portas de Santo Antão ❺

SEE ALSO

• *Street Life p25*

KEY

Ⓜ	Metro station
🚉	Railway station
⛴	Ferry boarding point
🚡	Funicular
ℹ	Tourist information

0 metres	500
0 yards	500

◀ *19th-century monument in the Praça dos Restauradores*

Jardim Botânico ❶

Map G4. Rua da Escola Politécnica 58. **Gardens** Open daily. Adm charge. **Museu de História Natural** Open Tue–Sun (times vary). Adm charge. **Museu de Ciência** Open Tue–Sun (times vary). Adm charge.

The complex, owned by the university of Lisbon, comprises two museums and four hectares (10 acres) of gardens. The botanical gardens have a distinct air of neglect. However, it is worth paying just to wander among the exotic trees and dense paths of the gardens as they descend from the main entrance towards Rua da Alegria. A magnificent avenue of lofty palms connects the two levels. The buildings at the top of the garden now house various museums, including the Museu de História Natural (Natural History Museum) and the Museu de Ciência (Science Museum) whose exhibits demonstrate basic key scientific principles.

Detail from the World War I memorial in Avenida da Liberdade

Avenida da Liberdade ❷

Map G4.

Following the earthquake of 1755, the Marquês de Pombal created the Passeio Público (public promenade) in the area now occupied by the lower part of Avenida da Liberdade and Praça dos Restauradores. Originally, enjoyment of the park was restricted to Lisbon's high society and walls ensured the exclusion of the lower classes. In 1821, the Liberals pulled down the barriers and the Avenida and square became open to all.

The boulevard was built in 1879–82 in the style of the Champs-Elysées in Paris and the wide tree-lined avenue became a focus for festivities and demonstrations. A war memorial stands as a tribute to those who died in World War I. The avenue still retains a certain elegance, but it no longer makes for a peaceful stroll as it is now divided by seven lanes of traffic. Some of the original mansions have been preserved, but many of the Art Nouveau façades have given way to newer ones occupied by offices, hotels and shopping complexes.

Walled garden within the Jardim Botânico

Museu da Sociedade de Geografia ❸

Map H4. Rua das Portas de Santo Antão 100. Guided tours compulsory and by appointment.

This museum, located in the Geographical Society building, houses a rather idiosyncratic ethnographical collection brought back from Portugal's former colonies. On display are exhibits such as circumcision masks from Guinea Bissau, musical instruments and snake spears. Most of the exhibits are arranged along the splendid Sala Portugal.

Praça dos Restauradores ❹

Map G4–H4.

This square, distinguished by its soaring obelisk built in 1886, commemorates Portugal's liberation from the Spanish yoke in 1640. The bronze figures on the pedestal depict Victory and Freedom. The names and

The imposing obelisk in the centre of Praça dos Restauradores

dates that are inscribed on the sides of the obelisk are those of the battles of the War of Restoration.

On the west side of the square is the Palácio Foz, built by Francesco Savario Fabri in 1755–77 for the Marquês de Castelo-Melhor and renamed after the Marquês de Foz, who lived here during the 19th century. The Avenida Palace Hotel, on the southwest side of the square, was designed by José Lúis Monteiro (1849–1942), who also built Rossio railway station.

Rua das Portas de Santo Antão ❺

Map H4.

This long Lisbon street is partly pedestrianized and has food for all tastes. The legendary Gambrinus is next door to the Ginjinha Sem Rival bar. Between these extremes are many seafood restaurants with outdoor seating, plus the cheerful Bomjardim, the inimitable Solmar and Casa do Alentejo.

Igreja de São Domingos ❻

Map H4. Largo de São Domingos. Open daily.

One of Lisbon's oldest churches, the Igreja de São Domingos is one of its hardiest survivors. Built in 1242, it was damaged by earthqakes in 1531 and 1755, and ravaged by fire in 1959. The blackened interior helps you imagine the days when inquisition processions would begin here, to end with charred corpses.

Teatro Nacional Dona Maria II on Rossio, illuminated at night

Rossio **7**

Map H4.

Formerly called Praça de Dom Pedro IV, this large square has been Lisbon's nerve centre for six hundred years. During its history it has been the stage of bullfights, festivals, military parades and the burning of heretics in the Inquisition.

Centre stage is a statue of Dom Pedro IV, the first emperor of independent Brazil. In the mid-19th century, the square was paved with wave-patterned mosaics that gave it the nickname of "Rolling Motion Square". Today, only a small central section of the design survives. On the north side of Rossio is the Neo-Classical Teatro Nacional Dona Maria II, which was built in the 1840s and named after Dom Pedro's daughter. The interior was destroyed by fire in 1964 and rebuilt in the 1970s. On top of the pediment is Gil Vicente (1465–1536), the founder of Portuguese theatre. Café Nicola on the west side of the square was a favourite meeting place among writers, including the poet Manuel du Bocage (1765–1805). Café Suiça, on the opposite side, is popular for its sunlit terrace.

Praça da Figueira **8**

Map H4.

Before the 1755 earthquake, the square next to Rossio was the site of the Hospital de Todos-os-Santos (All Saints). In the rebuilding programme that followed the quake, the square took on the role of the city's central marketplace. In 1885, a covered market was introduced, but this was pulled down in the 1950s. Today, the four-storey buildings are given over to

Bronze statue of King João I in Praça da Figueira

hotels, shops and cafés. Watch out for the multitude of pigeons that perch on the pedestal supporting the bronze equestrian statue of João I, erected in 1971.

Café on the top platform of the Elevador de Santa Justa

Elevador de Santa Justa ⑨

Map H5. Rua de Santa Justa and Largo do Carmo. Open daily. Adm charge.

Also called the Elevador do Carmo, this Neo-Gothic lift was built at the turn of the 20th century by the French architect Raoul Mesnier du Ponsard, an apprentice of Alexandre Gustave Eiffel. Made of iron, it is one of the more eccentric features of the Baixa. Passengers can travel up and down inside the tower in one of two wood-panelled cabins that each hold 25 people. There is also a walkway that links the lift with the Largo do Carmo in the Bairro Alto, 32 m (105 ft) above. The very top of the tower, which is reached via a tight spiral stairway, is given over to café tables. This high point commands splendid views of Rossio, the grid pattern

of the Baixa, the castle on the opposite hill, the river and the nearby ruins of the Carmo church. The fire that gutted the Chiado district in 1988 was extinguished very close to this lift.

Rua Augusta ⑩

Map H5.

Rua Augusta is a lively pedestrianized street decorated with mosaic pavements and lined with boutiques and open-air cafés. It is the main tourist thoroughfare and the smartest in the Baixa.

The other main streets of the Baixa are Rua da Prata (silversmiths' street) and Rua do Ouro or Rua Aurea (goldsmiths' street). Cutting across these main thoroughfares full of shops and banks are smaller streets that give glimpses up to the Bairro Alto to the west and the Castelo de São Jorge (*see pp12–13*) to the east. In the heart of the Baixa, located in Rua dos Correeiros, is a small section of the Roman baths. You can see the ruins and mosaics from the street or you can book a visit by phoning 211 131 004.

Shoppers on the lively and popular Rua Augusta

Núcleo Arqueológico da Rua dos Correeiros ⑪

Map H5. Rua dos Correeiros 9. Open 3–5pm Thu; 10am–12noon, 3–5pm Sat. Adm free.

When a Portuguese bank (now Millennium BCP) set about renovating its head office in the early 1990s, the builders' jackhammers unearthed ancient remnants of Roman Lisbon. A small museum was set up, and the digging goes on. So far, this has revealed parts of what appears to have been a riverside factory for making *garum*, the fermented fish sauce much loved by the Romans. A section of mosaic floor uncovered in a separate structure suggests other, or later uses.

Nossa Senhora da Conceição Velha ⑫

Map H5. Rua da Alfândega. Open daily (times vary).

The elaborate Manueline doorway is the only feature that survived from the original 16th-century church, Nossa Senhora da Misericórdia, which stood here until the massive 1755 earthquake. It was Manual I's sister, Queen Leonor, who founded the original almshouses here on the site of a former synagogue. Enjoyment of the portal is hampered by the traffic along Rua da Alfândega and the cars parked in front of the church. Inside, in one of the chapels, is a statue of Our Lady of Restelo, which came from the Belém chapel where navigators prayed before setting sail.

Praça do Comércio ⑬

Map H5.

More commonly known as Terreiro do Paço (Palace Square), this huge open space was the site of the royal palace for 400 years. The palace was destroyed in the earthquake of 1755 and Pombal's new palace occupied arcaded buildings that extended around three sides of the square.

The south side, graced by two square towers, looks across the River Tagus and has always been the finest gateway to Lisbon, where royalty and ambassadors would alight and take the steps up from the river. In the centre of the square is a statue of King José I on horseback erected in 1775 by Machado de Castro, the leading Portuguese sculptor of the 18th century.

The impressive triumphal arch on the north side of the square leads into Rua Augusta and is the gateway

Shaded arcades along the north side of Praça do Comércio

to the Baixa. Opened in 2001, in the northwest of the square, the Lisboa Welcome Centre has a gallery, shops, restaurants and a tourist information service. In the opposite corner is Lisbon's oldest café, the Martinho da Arcada, formerly a haunt of the city's literati. For many years the area was a car park, but today this is a vast open space used for cultural events and festivals.

STREET LIFE

RESTAURANTS

Casa do Alentejo
Map H4. Rua das Portas de Santo Antão 58. Tel 213 405 140.
Cheap
Beautiful Moorish-style tiled courtyard restaurant serving regional fare. Exhibitions and recitals often take place here.

Bonjardim Rei dos Frangos
Map H4. Travessa de Santo Antão 7–11. Tel 213 427 424.
Cheap
One of the best places for the Portuguese classic dish – grilled chicken with piri-piri.

Muni
Map H5. Rua dos Correeiros 115–117. Tel 218 884 203.
Moderate
Delightful restaurant serving traditional Portuguese food.

Solar dos Presuntos
Map H4. Rua das Portas de Santo Antão 150. Tel 213 424 253.
Moderate
Well known for its cured ham as well as its seafood dishes.

O Bacalhoeiro
Map H5. Rua dos Sapateiros 224. Tel 213 431 415.
Moderate
Cosy restaurant named after the Portuguese cod trawlers.

See p80 for price codes.

Gambrinus
Map H4. Rua das Portas de Santo Antão 23. Tel 213 421 466.
Expensive
One of the best seafood restaurants in the country.

CAFÉS AND BARS

Nicola
Map H4. Praça Dom Pedro IV 24.
Rossio's premier outdoor café is good for people-watching.

Confeitaria Nacional
Map H4. Praça da Figueira 18.
A Lisbon institution selling Portuguese cakes and pastries.

A Ginjinha
Map H4. Largo de São Domingos 8.
Ginjinha is Portuguese cherry liqueur and this tiny bar serves virtually nothing else.

SHOPPING

Discoteca Amália
Map H5. Rua do Ouro 272.
Specializes in traditional Portuguese music.

Joalharia Correia
Map H5. Rua do Ouro 245–7.
Jeweller's that cuts, replaces and repairs gems.

Manuel Tavares
Map H4. Rua da Betesga 1.
A good deli where you can try before you buy.

BAIRRO ALTO AND ESTRELA

The hilltop Bairro Alto is one of Lisbon's most picturesque districts. Its small workshops and family-run restaurants exist alongside a thriving nightlife. Very different to this is Chiado – the elegant commercial district where affluent Lisboetas do their shopping. The Estrela quarter centres on the basilica and gardens, while Lapa is home to foreign embassies and smart residences.

SIGHTS AT A GLANCE

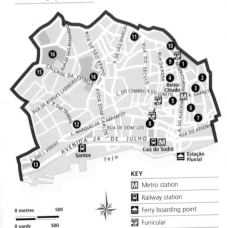

KEY

M	Metro station
🚉	Railway station
⛴	Ferry boarding point
🚡	Funicular

0 metres	500
0 yards	500

◀ Art Nouveau decoration in the Chiado's Café Brasileira

Ruins of the 14th-century Igreja do Carmo seen from the Baixa

São Roque ❶

**Map G4. Largo Trindade Coelho.
Open daily (times vary). Museu
de Arte Sacra** Open Tue–Sun.
Adm charge.

São Roque's plain façade
belies a remarkably rich
interior. The church was
founded at the end of the
16th century by the Jesuit
Order. In 1742, the Chapel
of St John the Baptist was
commissioned by João V
from the Italian architects
Luigi Vanvitelli and Nicola
Salvi. Constructed in Rome
and embellished with semi-
precious stones, gold, silver
and mosaics, the chapel was
given the Pope's blessing
then dismantled and sent
to Lisbon by ship.

Among the many tiles in
the church, the oldest and
most interesting are those in
the chapel dedicated to São
Roque (St Roch), protector
against the plague. The
church also features scenes
of the Apocalypse painted
on the ceiling and sacristy,
as well as painted panels of
the life of St Francis Xavier,
the 16th-century missionary.
Treasures from the Chapel of
St John are in the adjoining
Museu de Arte Sacra.

Igreja do Carmo ❷

**Map H5. Largo do Carmo. Open
Mon–Sat. Adm charge.**

The Gothic ruins of this
Carmelite church are an
evocative reminder of the
devastation left by the
earthquake of 1755. As the
congregation was attending
mass, the great shockwaves
caused the church to
collapse, depositing tons of
masonry on to the people
below. Founded in the
late 14th century by Nuno
Álvares Pereira, the military
commander who became a
member of the Carmelite
Order, the church was once
the biggest in Lisbon.

Nowadays the main body
of the church and the
chancel, whose roof
withstood the earthquake,
house an archaeological
museum with a small
heterogeneous collection
of sarcophagi, statuary,
ceramics and mosaics.
Among the more ancient
finds from Europe are a
remnant from a Visigothic
pillar and a Roman tomb.
Outside the ruins, in the
Largo do Carmo, stands the
Chafariz do Carmo, an
18th-century fountain.

Chiado ❸

Map G5–H5.

Chiado is now an elegant shopping district but it was once the haunt of writers and intellectuals. One fine reminder of its past is the statue of Fernando Pessoa, Portugal's most famous 20th-century poet, who is seated at a table outside the Café Brasileira. Established in the 1920s, this café was favoured by literary figures.

The name Chiado is often used to mean just Rua Garrett, the main shopping street of the area, named after the author and poet João Almeida Garrett (1799–1854). This elegant street, which descends from Largo do Chiado towards the Baixa, is known for its clothes shops, cafés and bookshops. Devastated by fire in 1988, the former elegance of this quarter has been recently restored.

On Largo do Chiado stand two Baroque churches: the Italian church, Igreja do Loreto, on the north side and opposite, Nossa Senhora da Encarnação, whose exterior walls are partly decorated with tiles (*azulejos*).

Zé dos Bois ❹

Map G5. Rua da Barroca 59. Open Wed–Sat.

ZDB, as it is also known, has consistently been Lisbon's most inspirational and genuinely "alternative" gallery. The Zé dos Bois is also a Bairro Alto bar.

Praça Luís de Camões ❺

Map G5.

This square, where Chiado meets Bairo Alto, is a favourite rendezvous. It is named after the famous 16th-century poet laureate, whose heroic bronze, with lesser chroniclers and colleagues in stone around his feet, presides over the bright white stone oval traffic island. It used to be shaded by magnificent umbrella pines, but these have now been replaced – supposedly for reasons of historical consistency – by still-puny poplars.

Art Nouveau façade of the popular Café Brasileira in the Chiado

Interior of the 18th-century Teatro Nacional de São Carlos

Teatro Nacional de São Carlos 6

Map G5. Rua Serpa Pinto 9. Open for performances.

Replacing an opera house that was ruined by the earthquake of 1755, the Teatro de São Carlos was built in 1792–5 by José da Costa e Silva. Designed on the lines of La Scala in Milan, the building has a beautifully proportioned façade and an enchanting Rococo interior. Unfortunately, views of the exterior are spoiled by the car park. The opera season lasts from September to June, but concerts and ballets are also staged here at other times of the year.

Museu do Chiado 7

Map H5. Rua Serpa Pinto 4–6. Open Tue–Sun. Adm charge.

The National Museum of Contemporary Art, whose collection of 1850–1950 works could no longer be called contemporary, changed its name in 1994 and moved to this stylishly restored warehouse. Each room has a different theme illustrating the development from Romanticism to Modernism. The majority of paintings and sculptures on display are by Portuguese artists. The few international works of art here include a collection of drawings by Rodin (1840–1917) and some late-19th-century French sculpture. There are also temporary exhibitions that are held for "very new artists, preferably inspired by the permanent collection".

Elevador da Bica 8

Map G5. Largo do Calhariz at Rua da Bica Duarte Belo. Runs daily (times vary). Bus/tram ticket.

Opened in 1892, this is the smallest of Lisbon's funiculars, passing through the lively neighbourhood of Bica on its way between Largo do Calhariz and Rua de São Paulo. Like Lisbon's other funiculars, it is powered by an electric motor, which moves the cable to which both cars are attached; they counterbalance each other and so lighten the motor's load.

Elevador da Bica – the smallest of Lisbon's funiculars

Solar do Vinho do Porto 9

Map G4. Rua de São Pedro de Alcântara 45. Open Mon–Sat.

The Portuguese word *solar* means mansion, or manor house, and the Solar do Vinho do Porto occupies the ground floor of an 18th-century mansion. The building was once owned by the German architect, Johann Friedrich Ludwig (Ludovice). The port wine institute of Oporto runs a pleasant, if dated, bar here for the promotion of port.

Miradouro de São Pedro de Alcântara 10

Map G4. Rua de São Pedro de Alcântara.

The belvedere *(miradouro)* commands a sweeping view of eastern Lisbon, seen across the Baixa. A tiled map, placed against the balustrade, helps you locate the landmarks below. Benches and ample shade from the trees make this terrace a pleasant stop after the steep walk up Calçada da Glória from the Baixa. Alternatively, the yellow funicular, Elevador da Glória, will drop you nearby.

The memorial in the garden, erected in 1904, depicts Eduardo Coelho (1835–89), founder of the newspaper Diário de Notícias, and a ragged paperboy.

The view is most attractive at sunset and by night when the castle is floodlit and the terrace becomes a meeting point for the young.

Local Lisboetas playing cards

Praça do Príncipe Real 11

Map G4.

Laid out in 1860 as a prime residential quarter, this square still retains an air of affluence. Smartly painted mansions surround a pleasant park with an open-air café, statuary and some splendid trees. The branches of a huge cedar tree have been trained on a trellis, creating a wide shady spot for the locals who play cards beneath it. On the large square, at No. 26, the eye-catching pink and white Neo-Moorish building is part of Lisbon University.

Museu da Marioneta 12

Map F5. Convento das Bernardas, Rua da Esperança 146. Open Tue–Sun. Adm charge.

This small puppet museum includes characters dating from 17th- and 18th-century theatre and opera. Many of the puppets possess contorted features that are unlikely to appeal to small children. The museum explains the history of the art form and runs videos of puppet shows. Call ahead to see if a performance is being held on the small stage.

Grotesque puppet in Museu da Marioneta

The sumptuous Baroque interior of the Chapel of St Albert

Museu Nacional de Arte Antiga ⓫

Map F5. Rua das Janelas Verdes. Tel 213 912 800. Open Tue–Sun (times vary). Adm charge (free 10am–2pm Sun).

Portugal's national art collection is housed in a 17th-century palace that was built for the counts of Alvor. In 1770, the palace was acquired by the Marquês de Pombal and it remained in his family's possession for over a century. The museum was opened in 1884 and an annexe (including the main façade) was added in 1940. This was built on the site of the the St Albert Carmelite monastery, which was partly demolished between 1910 and 1920. The only surviving feature is the chapel, which is now part of the museum.

Exploring the Collection

The museum has the largest collection of paintings in Portugal and is particularly strong on early religious works by Portuguese artists. The majority of exhibits came from convents and monasteries following the suppression of religious orders in 1834. There are also extensive displays of silverware, applied arts, sculpture and porcelain giving an overview of Portuguese art from the Middle Ages to the 19th century, complemented by many fine European and Oriental pieces.

European Art

Paintings dating from the 14th to the 19th centuries are arranged chronologically on the ground floor. The painters best represented here are 16th-century German and Flemish artists, such as Hieronymus Bosch (1450–1516) and Albrecht Dürer (1471–1528). Italian and Portuguese painters are also featured in the European galleries.

The Mystic Marriage of St Catherine (1519) by Hans Holbein the Elder

Portuguese Painting and Sculpture

Many of the earliest works of art are by the Portuguese primitive painters who were influenced by the realistic detail of Flemish artists.

There had always been strong trade links between Portugal and Flanders, and in the 15th and 16th centuries several painters of Flemish origin, such as Frey Carlos of Évora, set up workshops in Portugal. Pride of place, however, goes to the São Vicente de Fora polyptych, the most important painting of 15th-century Portuguese art, and one that has become a symbol of national pride in the Age of Discovery.

Portuguese and Chinese Ceramics

The extensive collection of ceramics enables visitors to trace the evolution of Chinese porcelain and Portuguese faïence, and to see the influence of oriental designs on Portuguese pieces, and vice versa. From the 16th century, Portuguese ceramics were being influenced by Chinese Ming. By the mid-18th century, individual potters had begun to develop a personalized, European style, with popular, rustic designs. The collection also includes ceramics from Italy, Spain and the Netherlands.

Faïence violin

Oriental and African Art

This collection of ivories and furniture further illustrates the reciprocal influences of Portugal and her colonies. The 16th-century taste for the exotic gave rise to a huge demand for items such as carved ivory hunting horns from Africa. Look out for the fascinating Namban screens from the 16th and 17th centuries, showing the Portuguese trading in Japan.

Silver, Gold and Jewellery

Among the museum's fine collection of ecclesiastical treasures are King Sancho I's gold cross (1214) and the Belém monstrance (1506). Also on display here is the 16th-century Madre de Deus reliquary, which allegedly holds a thorn from the crown of Christ. The highlight of the foreign collection is a set of rare 18th-century silver tableware. The 1,200 pieces include finely decorated tureens, sauce boats and saltcellars. The many jewels on display came from the convents, originally donated by nobles and the wealthy bourgeoisie on entering holy orders.

Applied Arts

Furniture, tapestries, textiles, liturgical vestments and bishops' mitres are among the wide range of objects exhibited here. The furniture collection includes many Medieval and Renaissance pieces, as well as Baroque and Neo-Classical items from the reigns of King João V, King José and Queen Maria I. The textiles include bedspreads and tapestries (many of Flemish origin, such as the *Baptism of Christ*) as well as embroidered rugs and Arriolos carpets.

Neo-Classical façade and stairway of Palácio de São Bento

Palácio de São Bento 14

Map F4–F5. Largo das Cortes, Rua de São Bento. Guided tours by appt only (213 919 446).

Also known as the Assembleia da República, this white Neo-Classical building started life in the late 1500s as the Benedictine monastery of São Bento. After the dissolution of the religious orders in 1834, the building became the seat of the Portuguese Parliament, known as the Palácio das Cortes. The interior is suitably grandiose.

Basílica da Estrela 15

Map F4. Praça da Estrela. Open daily.

In the second half of the 18th century, Maria I, daughter of José I, vowed she would build a church if she bore a son and heir to the throne. Her wish was granted and construction of the basilica began in 1779. Her son José, however, died of smallpox two years before the completion of the church in 1790. The huge domed basilica, set on a hill in the west of the city, is one of Lisbon's great landmarks. This church was built by architects from the Mafra School in late Baroque and Neo-Classical style. The façade is flanked by twin bell towers and decorated with an array of statues of saints and allegorical figures.

The spacious interior is clad in grey, yellow and pink marble. The elaborate Empire-style tomb of Queen Maria I, who died in Brazil, lies in the right transept. Locked in a room nearby is Machado de Castro's extraordinary Nativity scene, composed of over 500 cork and terracotta figures.

Jardim da Estrela 16

Map F4. Praça da Estrela. Open 7am–midnight daily.

Laid out in the middle of the 19th century, the popular gardens are a focal part of the Estrela quarter. Local families congregate here at weekends to enjoy the surroundings and sit at the café. The central feature of the park is a green wrought-iron bandstand where musicians strike up in the summer. The English Cemetery to the north is best known as the burial place of Henry Fielding (1707–54), the English novelist and playwright, who died in Lisbon at the age of 47.

The tomb of the pious Maria I in the Basílica da Estrela

STREET LIFE

RESTAURANTS

Associação Católica Internacional ao Serviço da Juventude Feminina
Map H5. Travessa do Ferragial 1 (top floor). Tel 213 240 910.
Cheap
A small rooftop terrace that has great views of Lisbon. An excellent lunch hideaway.

Bota Alta
Map G4. Travessa da Queimada 35. Tel 213 427 959.
Moderate
Traditional menu served in a restaurant located in the heart of Lisbon's bohemian quarter.

Casanostra
Map G5. Travessa do Poço da Cidade 60. Tel 213 425 931.
Moderate
Italian restaurant favoured by artists and intellectuals.

Pap'Açorda
Map G5. Rua da Atalaia 57. Tel 213 464 811.
Expensive
One of Lisbon's gastronomic landmarks serving modern Portuguese food.

Tavares Rico
Map G5. Rua da Misericórdia 35–37. Tel 213 421 112.
Expensive
Modern, international gourmet cuisine served in 18th-century surroundings.

CAFÉS AND BARS

Bénard
Map H5. Rua Garrett 104.
Tearoom with cakes and pastries superior to those of its neighbour, A Brasileira.

Vertigo
Map H5. Travessa do Carmo 4.
Old-fashioned café but with service and organic snacks that are bang up-to-date.

Portas Largas
Map G4. Rua Atalaia 105.
A rustic tavern-turned-bar that is predominantly gay, but not exclusively.

Artis
Map G5. Rua Diário de Notícias 95.
Great place for those who like low lights, the sound of jazz, late conversation and toasted chicken sandwiches.

Clube da Esquina
Map G5. Rua da Barroca 30.
On the way to classic status, this is a chatty, crowded, relaxed place. A good place to start a Bairro Alto night out.

SHOPPING

Ana Salazar
Map H5. Rua do Carmo 87.
Hailing from Lisbon, Ana Salazar is an internationally acclaimed stylist.

Vista Alegre
Map G5. Largo do Chiado 20–21.
A wide-ranging collection from Portugal's premier porcelain maker.

Agência 117
Map G5. Rua do Norte 117.
One of the first alternative fashion shops in Lisbon is a place both for browsing and hanging out.

See p80 for price codes.

BELÉM

Lying at the mouth of the River Tagus, Belém is a spacious, relatively green suburb with many museums, parks and gardens, as well as an attractive riverside setting with cafés and a promenade. On sunny days there is a distinct seaside feel to the river embankment, although the busy Avenida da Índia cuts central Belém off from the picturesque waterfront.

SIGHTS AT A GLANCE

Museums and Galleries
Museu de Arte Popular ⑩
Museu de Marinha ⑦
Museu Nacional de
  Arqueologia ⑤
Museu Nacional dos
  Coches ①
Planetário Calouste
  Gulbenkian ⑥

Parks and Gardens
Jardim Agrícola Tropical ③
Jardim Botânico da Ajuda ⑭

Monuments
Monument to the
  Discoveries ⑨

Cultural Centres
Centro Cultural
  de Belém ⑧

Churches and Monasteries
Ermida de São Jerónimo ⑫
Igreja da Memória ⑬
*Mosteiro dos Jerónimos
  pp40–41* ④

Historic Buildings
Palácio de Belém ②
Palácio Nacional da Ajuda ⑮
Torre de Belém p43 ⑪

SEE ALSO

• *Street Life p45*

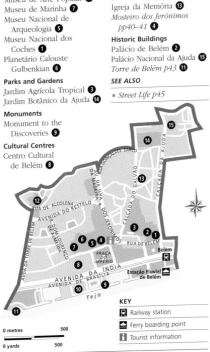

KEY	
🚉	Railway station
⛴	Ferry boarding point
ℹ	Tourist information

0 metres	500
0 yards	500

▼ *The distinctive Moorish watchtowers of the Torre de Belém*

Museu Nacional dos Coches ❶

Map B6. Praça Afonso de Albuquerque. Open Tue–Sun. Adm charge (free until 2pm Sun).

The museum's collection of coaches is arguably the finest in Europe. Occupying the east wing of the Palácio de Belém, this was formerly the riding school built by the Italian architect Giacomo Azzolini in 1726. Seated in the upper gallery, the royal family used to watch their beautiful Lusitanian horses performing in the arena. In 1905, King Carlos's wife, Dona Amélia, turned the riding school into a museum. The coaches on display span three centuries, and range from the plain to the utterly preposterous.

Palácio de Belém ❷

Map B6. Praça Afonso de Albuquerque. Open Sat (4pm–5pm). Guided tour compulsory (213 414 660). **Museum** Open Tue–Sun. Adm charge.

Built in 1559, before the Tagus had receded, this palace once had gardens bordering the river. In the 18th century it was bought by João V, who radically

Pink façade of the Palácio de Belém, home of the President of Portugal

altered it. At the time of the earthquake in 1755, King José I was staying here and so survived the devastation of central Lisbon. Today, the elegant pink building is the residence of the President of Portugal. A new museum, the Museu da Presidencia, has now opened on the premises of the palace.

The tranquil tropical gardens

Jardim Agrícola Tropical ❸

Map B6. Entrance in Largo dos Jerónimos. Open daily (times vary). Adm charge.

Also known as the Jardim do Ultramar, this peaceful park attracts surprisingly few visitors. Designed at the beginning of the 20th century as the research centre of the Institute for Tropical Sciences, it is more of an arboretum than a flower garden. The emphasis is on rare and endangered tropical and subtropical trees and plants. The Museu Tropical and research buildings are housed in the Palácio dos Condes da Calheta. The museum has 50,000 dried plant specimens and 2,414 samples of wood.

Mosteiro dos Jerónimos ❹

Map B6. See pp40–41.

Museu Nacional de Arqueologia ⑤

Map B6. Praça do Império.
Open Tue–Sun. Adm charge.

The long west wing of the Mosteiro dos Jerónimos *(see pp40–41)*, formerly the monks' dormitory, has been a museum since 1893. Reconstructed in the middle of the 19th century, the building is a poor imitation of the Manueline original. The museum now houses Portugal's main archaeological research centre and the exhibits are from sites all over the country.

Planetário Calouste Gulbenkian ⑥

Map A6. Praça do Império.
Open Thu (4pm), Sat (3pm) and Sun (3pm and 4pm).

Financed by the Gulbenkian Foundation *(see pp50–51)*, this modern building sits incongruously beside the Jerónimos monastery. Inside, the Planetarium reveals the mysteries of the cosmos. There are shows in Portuguese, English and French explaining the movement of the stars and our solar system, as well as presentations on more specialist themes, such as the constellations or the Star of Bethlehem (Belém).

Museu de Marinha ⑦

Map A6. Praça do Império.
Open Tue–Sun (times vary).
Adm charge.

The Maritime Museum was inaugurated in 1962 in the west wing of the Jerónimos monastery *(see p40–41)*. It

Façade of the Museu de Marinha

was here in the chapel that mariners took mass before embarking on their voyages. A hall devoted to the Discoveries illustrates the progress in shipbuilding from the mid-15th century, capitalizing on the experience of long-distance explorers. There are also navigational instruments, astrolabes and replicas of 16th-century maps showing the world as it was thought to be then. The stone pillars are replicas of the types of *padrão* set up as monuments to Portuguese sovereignty on the lands discovered.

A series of rooms displaying models of modern Portuguese ships leads on to the Royal Quarters, where you can see the exquisitely furnished wood-panelled cabin of King Carlos and Queen Amélia from the royal yacht *Amélia*, built in 1900. The modern, incongruous pavilion opposite houses original royal barges and the collection ends with a display of seaplanes.

Mosteiro dos Jerónimos ➍

A monument to the Age of Discovery, this monastery was commissioned by Manuel I in around 1501, after Vasco de Gama's return from his historic voyage to India. One of the most notable masterbuilders who worked on it was Diogo Boitac. The Order of St Jerome cared for the monastery until 1834, when all religious orders were disbanded.

Tomb of Vasco da Gama

The refectory *walls are tiled with 18th-century azulejos. The panel at the northern end depicts the Feeding of the Five Thousand.*

Museu Nacional de Arqueologia

Gallery

The façade *of Portugal's greatest national monument showing the long Neo-Manueline west wing.*

The cloisters were completed in 1544. Delicate tracery and richly carved images decorate the arches and balustrades.

Chapterhouse

The spectacular vaulting in the church of Santa Maria is held aloft by slender octagonal pillars. These rise like palm trees to the roof creating a feeling of space and harmony.

Chancel

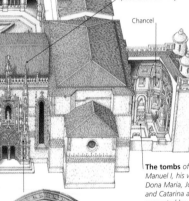

The tombs of Manuel I, his wife Dona Maria, João III and Catarina are supported by elephants.

The south portal's strict geometrical architecture is almost obscured by the elaborate decoration.

VISITORS' CHECKLIST

Map B6. Praça do Império. Tel 213 620 034. Open Tue–Sun (times vary). Adm charge (free 10am–2pm Sun).

Centro Cultural de Belém

Centro Cultural de Belém **8**

Map A6–A7. Praça do Império.
Berardo Collection Open daily.

Built as the headquarters of the Portuguese presidency of the European Community, this building opened as a cultural and conference centre in 1993. It stresses music, performing arts and photography. Half the building houses the Berardo Collection – one of the world's largest collections of modern and contemporary art, on rotating displays. Both the café and restaurant spill out onto the ramparts.

Monument to the Discoveries **9**

Map B7. Padrão dos Descobrimentos, Avenida de Brasília. Open daily (May–Sept); Tue–Sun (Oct–Apr). Adm for lift.

Standing prominently on the Belém waterfront, this huge monument was built in 1960 to mark the 500th anniversary of the death of the Henry the

Huge pavement compass in front of the Monument to the Discoveries

Navigator, who financed many worldwide trade explorations. The 52-m- (170-ft-) high monument is designed in the shape of a caravel. It commemorates the mariners, royal patrons and all those who took part in the development of Portugal's Age of Discovery. The huge mariner's compass cut into the paving stone was a present from the Republic of South Africa in 1960. The central map shows the routes of the discoverers in the 15th and 16th centuries. Inside the monument, a lift whisks you up to the sixth floor where steps then lead to the top for a splendid panorama of the river and Belém. The basement level is used for temporary exhibitions.

Museu de Arte Popular **10**

Map A7. Avenida de Brasília. Closed for renovation work.

This drab building houses the museum of Portuguese folk art and traditional handicrafts, and was opened in 1948. However, the museum is currently closed indefinitely for renovations. The exhibits, arranged by province, include pottery, costumes, agricultural tools, musical instruments, jewellery and brightly coloured saddles. The display gives a vivid indication of the diversity between the regions of Portugal. Each area has its speciality, such as the colourful ox yokes and ceramic cocks from the Minho, and cowbells and casseroles from the Alentejo.

Torre de Belém ⑪

Commissioned by Manuel I, the tower was built as a fortress in the middle of the Tagus in 1515–21. It was used as a starting point for the navigators who set out to discover the trade routes. The real beauty of the tower lies in the decoration of the exterior. Of note is the Gothic interior below the terrace, which once served as an arms store and a prison. In the tower, the private quarters are worth visiting for the loggia and the panorama.

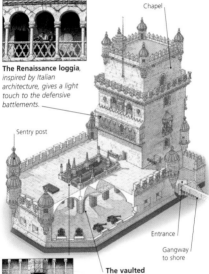

The Renaissance loggia, *inspired by Italian architecture, gives a light touch to the defensive battlements.*

Chapel

Sentry post

Entrance

Gangway to shore

The vaulted dungeon *was used as a prison until the 19th century.*

A Statue of Our Lady of Safe Homecoming *faces the sea, a symbol of protection for sailors.*

VISITORS' CHECKLIST

Map A7. Avenida da India. Tel 213 620 034. Open Tue–Sun (times vary). Adm charge (free Sun am).

The simple Manueline chapel, Ermida de São Jerónimo

Ermida de São Jerónimo ⑫

Map A6. Rua Pero de Covilhã. Open Mon–Fri (by appt only).

Also known as the Capela de São Jerónimo, this little chapel was built in 1514 when the influential architect Diogo Boitac was working on the Jerónimos monastery *(see pp40–41)*. Although far simpler than the monastery, it is also Manueline in style and may have been built to a design by Boitac. Perched on a quiet hill above Belém, the chapel has fine views down to the River Tagus and a path from the terrace outside the chapel winds down the hill towards the Torre de Belém.

Igreja da Memória ⑬

Map B6. Calçada do Galvão, Ajuda. Open for mass Mon–Sat (6pm), Sun (10am).

Built in 1760, this church was founded by King José I in gratitude for his escape from an assassination plot on this site in 1758. His chief minister, the Marquês de Pombal, used this as an excuse to get rid of his enemies in the Távora family, accusing them of conspiracy. In 1759, they were savagely tortured and executed. The Neo-Classical domed church has a marble-clad interior and a small chapel, on the right, containing the tomb of the Marquês de Pombal.

Jardim Botânico da Ajuda ⑭

Map B5. Calçada da Ajuda. Open daily (times vary). Adm charge.

Laid out on two levels by the Marquês de Pombal in 1768, these Italian-style gardens provide a respite from the noisy suburbs of Belém. Look out for the wrought-iron gates at the entrance as they are easy to miss. The park comprises about 5,000 plant species from America, Africa and Asia. Also of note is the 18th-century fountain decorated with fish, serpents, sea horses and mythical creatures, as well as the dragon tree, which is said to be about 400 years old. A terrace looks out over the lower level of the gardens.

Manicured formal gardens of the Jardim Botânico da Ajuda

Palácio Nacional da Ajuda ⑮

Map B5. Calçada da Ajuda. Open Thu–Tue. Adm charge (free Sun).

The royal palace, destroyed by fire in 1795, was replaced in the early 19th century by this Neo-Classical building. It was left incomplete when the royal family fled to Brazil in 1807, ahead of Napolean's invading army, and Rio de Janeiro temporarily became the capital of

19th-century throne from the Palácio Nacional da Ajuda

the large Portuguese empire. This palace only became a permanent residence of the royal family when Luís I became king of Portugal in 1861. On the first floor, the vast Banqueting Hall, with its silk-covered chairs, chandeliers and frescoed ceiling, is truly impressive. At the other end of the palace, the painting studio of Luís I, is a more intimate display of intricately carved furniture.

STREET LIFE

RESTAURANTS

Belém Terrace
Map A7. Avenida de Brasília, Doca de Belém.
Tel 213 620 865.
Moderate
Restaurant and bar with magnificent terrace serving unfussy food such as pasta.

Rosa dos Mares
Map B6. Rua de Belém 110.
Tel 213 621 811.
Moderate
Specialities here include wonderfully fresh seafood.

Ja Sei
Map A7. Avenida Brasília 202.
Tel 213 621 811.
Expensive
Situated on the edge of a lake with exquisite views and food.

Vela Latina
Map A7. Doca do Bom Sucesso. Tel 213 017 118.
Expensive
Idyllic waterfront location serving classic Portuguese cuisine.

CAFÉS AND BARS

Cafetaria Quadrante
Map A6–A7. Centro Cultural de Belém, Praça do Império.
Set in an attractive, minimalist garden within the Cultural Centre of Belém.

Antiga Confeitaria de Belém
Map B6. Rua de Belém 84–92.
Celebrated café and pastry shop famous for its custard tarts known locally as pastéis de Belém.

SHOPPING

Coisas do Arco do Vinho
Map A6–A7. Centro Cultural de Belém.
Specialist wine shop with an impressive selection.

Velentim de Carvalho
Map A6–A7. Centro Cultural de Belém.
One of a chain of music shops with outlets all over the city.

See p80 for price codes.

FURTHER AFIELD

The majority of the outlying sights, which include some of Lisbon's finest museums, are easily accessible by bus or metro from the city centre. A short walk north from Parque Eduardo VII brings you to the Calouste Gulbenkian Foundation and visitors with a spare half day can cross the Tagus to the huge Cristo Rei monument.

SIGHTS AT A GLANCE

Parks, Gardens and Zoos
Parque das Nações ⑪
Parque do Monteiro-Mor ⑮
Parque Eduardo VII ⑤
Oceanário de Lisboa ⑩

Architecture
Amoreiras Shopping
  Centre ③
Aqueduto das Águas
  Livres ⑬
Campo Pequeno ⑨

Cristo Rei ①
Palácio Fronteira ⑭
Ponte 25 de Abril ②
Praça Marquês de Pombal ④

Museums and Galleries
Centro de Arte Moderna ⑥
Museu Calouste
  Gulbenkian ⑦
Museu da Cidade ⑫
Museu Nacional do
  Azulejo ⑧

KEY

✈ Airport
⛴ Ferry boarding point
▬ Motorway
▬ Major road
▬ Minor road

0 kilometres   4
0 miles   2

◀ Tiled terrace leading to the chapel of the Palácio Fronteira

Cristo Rei overlooking the Tagus

Cristo Rei ❶

Santuário Nacional do Cristo Rei, Alto do Pragal, Almada. Open daily. Adm charge.

Modelled on the more famous Cristo Redentor in Rio de Janeiro, this giant-sized statue stands on the south bank of the Tagus. The 28-m- (92-ft-) tall figure of Christ was built by Francisco Franco in 1949–59. You can see the monument from various points in the city, but it is fun to take a ferry then a bus or taxi to the statue. A lift, plus some steps, takes you up 82 m (269 ft) to the top, giving fine views out over the city.

Ponte 25 de Abril ❷

Map D6–D7.

Originally called the Ponte Salazar after the dictator who had it built in 1966, Lisbon's

Ponte 25 de Abril linking Lisbon with the south bank of the Tagus

suspension bridge was renamed (like many other monuments) to commemorate the peaceful Carnation Revolution of 25 April 1974, which restored democracy to Portugal.

Inspired by San Francisco's Golden Gate Bridge in the United States, this huge steel construction stretches for 1 km (half-a-mile) and links central Lisbon with the Outra Banda, the south bank of the Tagus. In 1999, the lower tier was adapted to accommodate the Fertagus, a much-needed railway across the Tagus.

The bridge's notorious traffic congestion was partly resolved by the opening of the 11-km (7-mile) Vasco da Gama bridge in 1998. Named after the explorer, this bridge spans the river from Montijo to Sacavém, north of the Parque das Nações.

Amoreiras Shopping Centre ❸

Map F3. Avenida Engenheiro Duarte Pacheco. Open daily.

In the 18th century, the Marquês de Pombal planted mulberry trees *(amoreiras)* on the western edge of the city to create food for silk worms. Hence the name of the futuristic shopping centre that was built here in 1985. This vast complex, with pink and blue towers, houses 370 shops, ten cinemas and numerous restaurants. Once an incongruous feature, it now draws the crowds, particularly the young, and has been joined by other new buildings and shopping centres in the area.

Tropical plants in one of the glasshouses in Parque Eduardo VII

Praça Marquês de Pombal ④

Map G3.

At the top of the Avenida da Liberdade (*see p20*), traffic roars around the "Rotunda" (roundabout), as the square is also known. At the centre is the lofty monument to the despotic chief minister, the Marquês de Pombal, who virtually ruled Portugal in 1750–77. He stands on the top of the column, his hand on a lion (symbol of power) and his eyes directed down to the Baixa, whose creation he masterminded. Although greatly feared, this dynamic politician propelled Portugal into the Age of Enlightenment. An underpass, which is not always open, leads to the centre of the square. Nearby, the well-tended Parque Eduardo VII extends northwards behind the square. The paving stones around the Rotunda are decorated with a mosaic of Lisbon's coat of arms. Similar patterns decorate many of the city's streets and squares.

Parque Eduardo VII ⑤

Map F3–G3. Praça Marquês de Pombal.

The largest park in central Lisbon was named in honour of King Edward VII of the United Kingdom who came to Lisbon in 1902 to reaffirm the Anglo-Portuguese alliance. The wide grassy slope, which extends for 25 hectares (62 acres), was laid out as Parque da Liberdade, a continuation of Avenida da Liberdade (*see p20*), in the late 19th century. Neat box hedging, flanked by patterned walkways, extends uphill to a belvedere. From here, there are fine views of the city. The most inspiring parts of this rather monotonous park are the hot and cold glasshouses although they are currently closed. Near them, a pond with carp and a galleon-shaped play area are popular with children. On the east side, the Pavilhão Carlos Lopes is used for concerts and conferences.

Centro de Arte Moderna ⑥

Map F2. Rua Dr Nicolau de Bettencourt. Open Tue–Sun. Adm charge.

The Modern Art Museum lies across the gardens from the Calouste Gulbenkian Museum and is part of the same cultural foundation (*see pp50–51*). The collection features paintings and sculpture by Portuguese artists from the turn of the 20th century to the present day. The museum is light and spacious, with pleasant gardens and a busy cafeteria.

Egyptian bronze cat and kittens dating from around the 7th century BC

Museu Calouste Gulbenkian ❼

Map F2. Avenida de Berna 45.
Open Tue–Sun. Adm charge
(free Sun).

Thanks to a wealthy Armenian oil magnate, Calouste Gulbenkian, with wide-ranging tastes and an eye for a masterpiece, this museum has one of the finest collections of art in Europe. Inaugurated in 1969, the purpose-built museum was created as part of the charitable institution bequeathed to Portugal by the multimillionaire. The design of the building, set in a spacious park allowing natural light to fill some of the rooms, was devised to create the best layout for the founder's varied art collection.

Exploring the Collection

Housing Calouste Gulbenkian's unique collection of art, this museum ranks with the Museu de Arte Antiga (*see pp32–3*) as one of the finest collections in Lisbon. The exhibits, which span over 4,000 years, from ancient Egyptian statuettes through

Chinese porcelain vase

Islamic glassware, to Art Nouveau brooches, are displayed in spacious and well-lit galleries, many overlooking the gardens or courtyards. The museum is quite small, but each work of art is worthy of attention.

Egyptian, Classical and Mesopotamian Art

Priceless treasures chart the evolution of Egyptian art from the Old Kingdom (c.2700 BC) to the Roman Period (1st century BC). The exhibits range from an alabaster bowl of the 3rd Dynasty to a surprisingly modern-looking statuette of *Venus Anadyomene* from the Roman period.

Oriental Islamic Art

Being Armenian, Gulbenkian had a keen interest in art from the Near and Middle East. The Oriental Islamic gallery has a fine collection of Persian and Turkish carpets, textiles and ceramics, while the Armenian section has some exquisite illustrated manuscripts produced by Armenian refugees in Istanbul, Persia and the Crimea during the 16th to 18th centuries.

Far Eastern Art
Gulbenkian acquired a large collection of Chinese porcelain between 1910 and 1930. One of the rarest pieces is the blue-glazed bowl from the Yüan Dynasty (1279–1368). Most of the exhibits are the later *famille verte* porcelain and the K'ang Hsi biscuitware of the 17th and 18th centuries.

European Art (14th–17th centuries)
Illuminated manuscripts, printed books and medieval ivories introduce

The graceful Diana, goddess of the hunt

the section on Western art. The collection of early European paintings progresses to Flemish and Dutch works of the 17th century, including two works by Rembrandt. The gallery beyond the Dutch and Flemish paintings has tapestries and textiles from Italy and Flanders, Italian ceramics, rare 15th-century medals and sculpture.

French 18th-century Decorative Arts
Some remarkably elaborate Louis XV and Louis XVI pieces, many commissioned by royalty, feature in the collection of French 18th-century furniture. The exhibits are grouped by historical style, with Beauvais and "chinoiserie" Aubusson tapestries

decorating the walls. Much of the French silverware, which is shown here from the same period, once adorned the dining tables of imperial Russian palaces.

European Art (18th–19th centuries)
The 18th century art is dominated by French painters, including Watteau (1684–1721), Boucher (1703–70) and Fragonard (1832–1806). The most famous of all the sculptures is that of *Diana* by Jean-Antoine Houdon. It was executed in 1780 and became one of the main exhibits in the Hermitage in Russia during the 19th and 20th centuries. French 19th-century landscape painting is well represented here, reflecting Gulbenkian's preference for naturalism.

Lalique Collection
The tour of the museum ends with an entire room filled with the flamboyant creations of French Art Nouveau jeweller, René Lalique (1860–1945). Gulbenkian was a close friend of Lalique's and he acquired many of the pieces of jewellery, glassware and ivory on display here directly from the artist. Inlaid with semi-precious stones and covered with enamel or gold leaf, the pieces feature typical Art Nouveau motifs, such as animals.

A striking 18th-century panel in the Museu Nacional do Azulejo

Museu Nacional do Azulejo ⓼

Rua da Madre de Deus 4. Open Tue–Sun (times vary). Adm charge (free 10am–2pm Sun).

Part of a 16th-century pottery altarpiece

Dona Leonor, widow of King João II, founded the Convento da Madre de Deus in 1509. Originally built in Manueline style, the church was restored under João III using simple Renaissance designs. The striking Baroque decoration was added by João V. The convent cloisters provide a stunning setting for the National Tile Museum. Individual tiles, decorative panels and photographs trace the evolution of tilemaking from its introduction by the Moors to Spanish influence and the development of Portugal's own style up to the present day.

The convent's church, Madre de Deus, was completed in the mid-16th century, but it was not until two centuries later that the church acquired its ornate decoration. The Rococo altarpiece was added after the earthquake in 1755.

An important surviving feature of the original convent is the graceful Manueline cloister. The fine geometrically patterned tiles were added to the cloister walls in the 17th century.

Gallery Guide

The rooms around the central cloister are arranged chronologically, with the oldest tiles on the ground floor. Access to the Madre de Deus is via Level 2 of the museum. This is because the front entrance of the church is used only during religious services.

The ornate Baroque interior of the Madre de Deus church

Campo Pequeno ⑨

Map G1. Shopping Centre
Open 10am–11pm daily. **Bullring**
Open for bullfights and other
events (May–Oct). Adm charge.

This square is dominated by
the red-brick Neo-Moorish
bullring built in the late 19th
century. The building, known
as the Campo Pequeno
Complex, has recently
undergone major develop-
ment work although much
of the bullring's distinctive
architecture remains. The
complex now functions
primarily as a shopping
centre, while the arena is a
regular venue for shows and
concerts as well as bullfights.

*Neo-Moorish façade of the bullring
in Campo Pequeno*

Oceanário de Lisboa ⑩

Esplanada D. Carlos 1, Parque das
Nações. Open daily (times vary).
Adm charge.

Centrepiece of Expo '98
and now the main attraction
at Parque das Nações, the
oceanarium was designed
by American architect Peter
Chermayeff. It is the second-
largest aquarium in the
world, and holds a vast array
of species – birds and some
mammals as well as fish and
other underwater dwellers.
The main attraction for most
visitors is the impressive
central tank with its dazzling
variety of fish.

Parque das Nações ⑪

Avenida Dom João II. Open daily.
**Pavilhão do Conhecimento–
Ciencia Viva** Open Tue–Sun
(times vary). Adm charge. **Casino
Lisboa** Open daily (times vary).
Cable car Open daily. Adm charge.

Originally the site of Expo
'98, Parque das Nações has
become a new focus for
Lisbon. With its modern
living spaces, contemporary
architecture and family-
oriented attractions, the park
has revitalized the eastern
waterfront. The impressive
Portugal Pavilion has an
enormous reinforced-
concrete roof suspended
above its forecourt.
    The Casino Lisboa opened
in 2006, and features a
spacious area for gaming
tables spread over two
floors. It also contains the
Oceanos Auditorium, which
presents leading performing
arts productions.
    The Pavilhão do
Conhecimento–Ciencia Viva
(Knowledge and Science
Pavilion) is a science
museum that has several
interactive exhibitions.
Spectacular views can be
had from Lisbon's tallest
building, the Torre Vasco da
Gama, and the cable car that
connects the Torre Vasco da
Gama with the marina.
Visitors to the Parque can
stroll along the promenade
by the river or visit the Sony
Plaza and Pavilhão Atlantico,
which are located nearby.

Museu da Cidade ⑫

Campo Grande 245. Open
Tue–Sun. Adm charge
(free Sun).

Palácio Pimenta
was allegedly
commissioned
by João V for his
mistress, Madre
Paula, a nun
from the nearby
convent at
Odivelas. When
the mansion
was built, in the
middle of the 18th
century, it occupied
a peaceful site outside the
capital. Nowadays it has to
contend with the traffic of
Campo Grande. The house
itself, however, retains its
period charm and the city
museum is one of the most
interesting in Lisbon.

The displays follow the
development of the city
from prehistoric times
through to the Romans,
Visigoths and Moors, traced
by means of tiles, drawings,
paintings, models and
historical documents. Some
of the most fascinating
exhibits are those depicting
Lisbon before the massive
earthquake of November
1755, including a detailed
model made in the 1950s.

*18th-century
Indian toy*

Aqueduto das Águas Livres ⑬

Best seen from Calçada da
Quintinha. Open Mon–Sat.
**Mãe d'Água das
Amoreiras** Praça
das Amoreiras.
Open Mon–Sat.

The Aqueduto das
Águas Livres looms
over the Alcântara
valley, northwest of
the city. The building
of an aqueduct gave
João V the opportunity
to indulge his passion
for grand building
schemes, as the only area of
Lisbon with fresh drinking
water was the Alfama.
Although not complete until
the 19th century, it was
already supplying the city
with water by 1748.

The main pipeline
measures 19 km (12 miles),
but the total length is 58 km
(36 miles). The most visible
parts of this structure are
the 35 arches, the tallest of
which rise to 65 m (213 ft)
above the ground. The
walkway along the aqueduct
has been closed since 1853,
although it is possible to
take a guided tour over the
arches. There are also tours
of the Mãe d'Água reservoir
and trips to the Mãe d'Água

Imposing arches of the Aqueduto das Águas Livres

springs, the source of the water supply. At the end of the aqueduct, the Mãe d'Água das Amoreiras is a castle-like building that once served as a reservoir for the water from the aqueduct. Today the space is used for art exhibitions, fashion shows and other events. There are great views from the roof.

Palácio Fronteira ⑭

Largo São Domingos de Benfica 1. Open Mon–Sat. Adm charge.

This delightful country manor house was built as a hunting pavilion for João de Mascarenhas, the first Marquês de Fronteira, in 1640. Although skyscrapers are visible in the distance, it still occupies a quiet spot by the Parque Florestal de Monsanto. The palace is still occupied by the 12th Marquis, however, some of the living rooms and the library, as well as the formal gardens, are included in the guided tour.

The late 16th-century chapel is the oldest part of the house. The façade is adorned with stones, shells, glass and bits of china. These fragments of crockery are believed to have been used at the inauguration feast and then smashed to ensure no one else could sup off the same set. Visits to the garden start at the chapel terrace. In the formal Italian garden the immaculate box hedges are cut into shapes to represent the seasons of the year. On either side of the water, a grand staircase leads to a terrace above.

Entrance to the theatre museum in the Parque do Monteiro-Mor

Parque do Monteiro-Mor ⑮

Largo Júlio Castilho. **Park** Open Tue–Sun. **Museu Nacional do Traje** Open Tue–Sun. Adm charge. **Museu Nacional do Teatro** Open Tue–Sun (times vary). Adm charge.

Monteiro-Mor Park was sold to the state in 1975 and the 18th-century palace buildings were converted to museums. The gardens are attractive and more romantic than the manicured box-hedge gardens so typical of Lisbon, and much of the land is wooded. The Museu Nacional do Traje (Costume Museum) exhibits textiles, accessories and costumes worn by poets, musicians, politicians, aristocrats and soldiers. The Museu Nacional do Teatro (Theatre Museum) has one building for temporary exhibitions and another one with a permanent collection. Photographs, posters and cartoons feature famous 20th-century Portuguese actors, and one section is devoted to Amália Rodrigues, the Fado singer.

DAY TRIPS FROM LISBON

To the north, the beautiful hill town of Sintra is dotted with palaces, while on the coast, cosmopolitan Cascais and the fishing town of Ericeira are both excellent bases from which to explore. South of the Tagus, the Serra da Arrábido and the rugged coast can be visited from Sesimbra. Inland, the nature reserves of the Tagus and Sado estuaries offer a quiet retreat.

SIGHTS AT A GLANCE

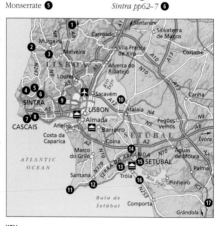

KEY

🚢 Ferry port

▬ Motorway

— Major road

— Regional border

0 kilometres   20

0 miles   10

◀ *Prala da Duquesa, Cascais, on the Estoril coast*

Alcobaça ❶

Portugal's largest church, the Mosteiro de Santa Maria de Alcobaça, is renowned for its simple medieval architecture. It was commissioned by King Afonso Henriques to commemorate a victory over the Moors in 1147, and it was completed in 1223. The monastery was further endowed by other monarchs, notably King Dinis, who built the main cloister in 1308.

The doorway of the sacristy is adorned with ornate foliage and elaborate pinnacles. This Manueline portal is attributed to João de Castilho.

Dormitory

The refectory is where the monks ate. Next door is the vast kitchen, housing a stream that provided the monks with a constant water supply.

The Cloister of Dom Dinis is also known as the Cloister of Silence and was ordered by King Dinis in 1308. The austere galleries and double arches are in keeping with Cistercian simplicity.

The tomb of Pedro I *is attended by angels. He lies facing the tomb of his beloved, Inês de Castro.*

The central nave's *vaulted roof and soaring columns create an impression of harmony and simplicity.*

Entrance

In the Sala dos Reis *(King's Hall), statues of Portuguese kings adorn the walls and tiled panels depict the founding of the abbey.*

The façade *is a richly decorated 18th-century addition. Marble statues of St Benedict and St Bernard flank the doorway.*

VISITORS' CHECKLIST

Santa Maria de Alcobaça, 137 km (85 miles) N of Lisbon. Tel 262 505 120. Open daily (times vary) – last adm: 30 mins before closing. Services: 11am Sun. Adm charge (free 9am–2pm Sun).

Tractor pulling a fishing boat out of the sea at Ericeira

Ericeira ❷

66 km (41 miles) NW of Lisbon.

Ericeira is an old fishing village that manages to keep its traditions despite an ever-increasing influx of summer visitors from Lisbon and abroad, who enjoy the bracing climate, clean, sandy beaches and fresh seafood. In July and August, the pavement cafés, restaurants and bars around the tree-lined Praça da República are buzzing late into the night. As well as the beach, attractions include a crazy golf course in Santa Marta park and a local history museum, the Museu da Ericeira, exhibiting model boats and traditional regional fishing equipment. The unspoilt old town, a maze of whitewashed houses and cobbled streets, is perched high above the ocean. From Largo das Ribas, at the top of a 30-m (100-ft) stone-faced cliff, there is a view over the busy fishing harbour below. On 16 August, the annual fishermen's festival is celebrated with a candlelit procession to the harbour for the blessing of the boats.

Palácio de Mafra ❸

55 km (34 miles) NW of Lisbon. Terreiro de Dom João V, Mafra. Open Wed–Mon. Adm charge.

This massive Baroque palace and monastery dwarfs the small town of Mafra. It was built during the reign of João V and began with a vow by the young king to build a new monastery and basilica. Work began in 1717 on a project to house 13 friars but the king and his architect, Johann Friedrich Ludwig (1670–1752), made ever more extravagant plans. In the end, the project housed not 13, but 330 friars, a royal palace and one of the best

Stunning library in the Palacio de Mafra, paved with chequered marble

Picturesque village of Azenhas do Mar, near Colares

libraries in Europe. Most of the finest furniture and art was taken to Brazil when the royal family escaped the French invasion in 1807. The monastery was abandoned in 1834 and the palace in 1910. A wolf conservation project is run here today.

Tours take in the monastery, pharmacy and hospital, the sumptuous palace state rooms and the domed basilica as well as Mafra's magnificent library.

Colares ❹

44 km (27 miles) W of Lisbon.

On the lower slopes of the Serra de Sintra, this lovely village faces towards the sea over a green valley. Small quantities of the famous Colares wine are still made and can be sampled at the Adega Regional de Colares.

There are several popular beach resorts west of Colares. From the village of Banzão you can ride 3 km (2 miles) to Praia das Maças on the old tramway, which runs from July to September. Just north of here is the pretty village of Azenhas do Mar, clinging to the cliffs; to the south is the larger resort of Praia Grande. The unspoilt village of Praia da Adraga, 1 km (half-a-mile) further south, has a delightful beach café and restaurant.

Monserrate ❺

34 km (21 miles) NW of Lisbon. Estrada de Monserrate. Open daily (times vary).

The wild, romantic garden of this once-magnificent estate is a jungle of exotic trees and flowering shrubs. The gardens were landscaped in the late 1700s by an Englishman, William Beckford. In 1856, another Englishman, Sir Francis Cook, bought the estate and built a fantastic Moorish-style palace (which now stands empty) and transformed the gardens with a large sweeping lawn, camellias and sub-tropical trees from all over the world.

Sadly neglected Moorish-style Palace of Monserrate

Sintra ⑥

31 km (19 miles) NW of Lisbon.

Sintra's stunning setting on the north slopes of the granite Serra, among wooded ravines and freshwater springs, made it a favourite summer retreat for the kings of Portugal.

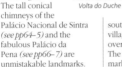

A tiled fountain on Volta do Duche

The tall conical chimneys of the Palácio Nacional de Sintra (*see pp64–5*) and the fabulous Palácio da Pena (*see pp66–7*) are unmistakable landmarks.

Today, the town draws thousands of visitors all through the year. Even so, there are many peaceful walks in the wooded hills around Sintra, which are especially beautiful in the long, cool evenings in the Portuguese summer.

Exploring Sintra

Present-day Sintra is in three parts, Sintra Vila, Estefânia and São Pedro, joined by a confusing maze of narrow winding roads scattered over the surrounding hills. In the pretty cobbled streets of the old town are the museums and beautifully tiled post office. The curving Volta do Duche leads from the old town north to the Estefânia district and the Neo-Gothic Câmara Municipal (Town Hall). To the south and east, the hilly village of São Pedro spreads over the slopes of the Serra. The fortnightly Sunday market here extends across the broad market square and along Rua 1° de Dezembro. Exploring Sintra on foot involves a lot of climbing up and down its steep hills. For a more leisurely tour, take one of the horse and carriage rides around the town. The Miradouro da Vigia in São Pedro offers impressive views, as does the cosy Casa de Sapa café, where you can sample *queijadas*, the local sweet.

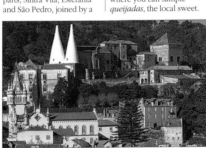

Chimneys of the Palácio Nacional de Sintra above the old town

Battlements of the Castelo dos Mouros on the slopes of the Serra

Museu do Brinquedo

Rua Visconde de Monserrate.
Open Tue–Sun. Adm charge.

This small museum has a fine collection of toys, ranging from model planes and dolls to clockwork models of cars and soldiers. There is also a restoration workshop and a playroom with puppets and storytellers.

Museu de Arte Moderna

Avenida Heliodoro Salgado.
Open Tue–Sun. Adm charge.

Located at the northern end of Sintra, this museum houses part of the Berardo Collection, gathered by entrepreneur Joe Berardo. It is regarded as one of the world's best private collections of 20th-century art, although some of the most important pieces have been moved to the museum at the Centro Cultural de Belém (see p42).

Quinta da Regaleira

Rua Barbosa du Bocage. Open daily (times vary). Guided tours mandatory. Adm charge.

Built in the 1890s, this palace and its gardens are a feast of historical and religious references, occult symbols and mystery.

Castelo dos Mouros

Avenida Heliodoro Salgado.
Open Tue–Sun. Adm charge.

Standing above the old town, the ramparts of the 8th-century Moorish castle snake over the top of the Serra. There are great views from the castle walls over the old town to Palácio da Pena (see pp66–7), on a neighbouring peak, and along the coast. Hidden inside the walls are a ruined chapel and an ancient Moorish cistern. A path threads up through wooded slopes from the 12th-century church of Santa Maria.

Parque da Pena

Estrada da Pena. Open daily (times vary).

A huge park surrounds the Palácio da Pena, and hidden away among the foliage are gazebos, fountains, follies and a Romantic chalet built by Fernando II for his mistress in 1869. Cruz Alta, at 530 m (1,740 ft), commands spectacular views of the Serra and surrounding plain.

*Toy Alfa Romeo,
Museu do Brinquedo*

Palácio Nacional de Sintra

At the heart of Sintra's old town lies the Royal Palace. The main part of the palace was built by João I in the late 14th century on a site once occupied by Moorish rulers. Additions to the palace by Manual I in the early 16th century echo the Moorish style. It became a favourite summer retreat for the court, and continued as a royal residence until the 1880s. Gradual rebuilding over the centuries has led to a fascinating mix of styles.

The Sala dos Brasões has a domed ceiling decorated with stags holding the coats of arms (brasões) of 72 noble Portuguese families.

The Sala dos Árabes is decorated with fine azulejos.

The Sala das Galés (galleons) houses temporary exhibitions.

Jardim da Preta (walled garden)

The Sala das Pegas has ceiling panels painted with magpies (pegas). Supposedly, they were painted to rebuke court women for gossiping like chattering magpies.

The Sala dos Cisnes *(Banqueting Hall)* has a splendid ceiling that was painted in the 15th century. It is divided into octagonal panels decorated with swans *(cisnes).*

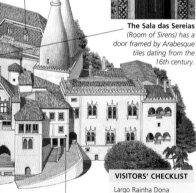

The kitchens *lie beneath two huge chimneys.*

Chapel

The Sala das Sereias *(Room of Sirens) has a door framed by Arabesque tiles dating from the 16th century.*

Sala dos Archeiros (entrance hall)

VISITORS' CHECKLIST

Largo Rainha Dona Amélia. Tel 219 106 840. Open 9:30am–5:30pm Thu–Tue. Last adm: 30 mins before closing. Adm charge (free 10am–2pm Sun).

Sintra: Palácio da Pena

On the highest peaks of the Serra de Sintra stands this spectacular palace – an eclectic medley of styles built in the 19th century for Queen Maria II's husband, Ferdinand Saxe-Coburg-Gotha. Ferdinand himself appointed the German architect Baron Von Eschwege to build a palace filled with oddities from all over the world surrounded by a park. In 1910, the palace became a museum, preserved as it was when the royal family lived here.

Manuel II's bedroom is decorated with green walls and has a stuccoed ceiling. A portrait of Manuel II, the last king of Portugal, hangs above the fireplace.

In the kitchen, the copper pots and utensils still hang around the iron stove.

The spacious ballroom is grandly furnished with stained-glass windows, precious Oriental porcelain and four torchbearers holding giant candelabra.

The altarpiece in the chapel was designed by the French sculptor Nicolau Chanterène.

The Arab Room's walls and ceiling are covered with marvellous frescoes, making this one of the loveliest rooms in the palace. The Orient was a great inspiration to Romanticism.

The Triton Arch is encrusted with Neo-Manueline decoration.

The cloister, decorated with colourful tiles, is part of the original monastery building.

A studded archway with turrets forms part of the entrance to the palace. The palace buildings are painted the original yellow and strawberry pink.

VISITORS' CHECKLIST

Estrada da Pena, 5 km (3 mile) S of Sintra. Tel 219 105 340. Open Tue–Sun (times vary) Adm charge.
www.parquesdesintra.pt

Outdoor café in the popular holiday resort of Cascais

Cascais ❼

32 km (20 miles) W of Lisbon.

The sandy, sheltered bay around which the modern town of Cascais has spread was a fishing harbour in prehistoric times. Fishing still goes on, but the town today is first of all a favoured suburb of Lisbon. Despite the ceaseless construction boom that has swept Cascais, the beautiful, windswept coastline beyond the town has been left relatively undeveloped.

The Museu do Conde de Castro Guimaraes is the best place to get a taste of the old holiday resort that grew up in the late 19th century. Across the road from the museum is the new marina, with its small shopping centre, restaurants and cafés. Worth visiting nearby are the Boca do Inferno (Mouth of Hell), where the sea rushes into clefts and caves in the rocks, and the magnificent sandy beach of Guincho.

Estoril ❽

27 km (17 miles) W of Lisbon.

Despite once being the haunt of exiled royalty fleeing European republicanism, the lovely town of Estoril does not rest on its historical laurels. Today it is a tourist and business resort, and a retirement haven. There are also a number of good golf courses nearby.

What separates Estoril from Cascais, besides a pleasant beach promenade of 3 km (2 miles) and a mansion-covered ridge known as Monte Estoril, is its sense of place. The heart of Estoril is immediately accessible from the train station. On one side of the tracks is the riviera-like beach, on the other, a park flanked by grand buildings, leading up past fountains to what is said to be Europe's biggest casino. Dwarfing the casino is the multipurpose Estoril Congress Centre.

Sandy beach and promenade along the bay of Estoril

Palácio de Queluz ❾

See pp70–71.

Alcochete ❿

36 km (22 miles) E of Lisbon.

This delightful old town overlooks the wide Tagus estuary from the southern shore. Salt has long been one of the main industries here, and saltpans can still be seen to the north and south of the town.

Statue of a salt worker in Alcochete (1985)

On the outskirts is a statue of Manuel I, who was born here on 1 June 1469 and granted the town a Royal Charter in 1515.

The Reserva Natural do Estuário do Tejo covers a vast area of estuary water, salt marshes and small islands around Alcochete and is a very important breeding ground for water birds, such as flamingos.

Cabo Espichel ⓫

47 km (29 miles) S of Lisbon.

Stunning views of the ocean and the coast can be enjoyed from this bleak outcrop of land, but beware of the strong gusts of wind on the cliff edge. In this desolate setting stands the impressive Santuário de Nossa Senhora do Cabo, a late-17th-century church with its back to the sea. On either side of the church is a long line of pilgrims' lodgings. These face inwards to form an open courtyard. Nearby, a domed chapel has blue and white *azulejo* panels depicting fishing scenes.

Sesimbra ⓬

38 km (24 miles) S of Lisbon.

A steep, narrow road leads down to this busy fishing village, which is a popular holiday resort with Lisboetas. It was occupied by the Romans and later the Moors until King Sancho II conquered its heavily defended forts in 1236. The old town is a maze of narrow streets, with the Santiago Fort in the centre overlooking the sea. From the terrace, there are views over the town, the Atlantic and the sandy beach. Sesimbra is fast developing as a resort, with holiday flats appearing on the surrounding hillsides, and plentiful pavement cafés and bars. The fishing fleet of brightly painted boats is moored in the Porto do Abrigo to the west of the main town. High above is the Moorish castle, greatly restored in the 18th century. There are wonderful views from the castle ramparts, especially at sunset.

Colourful fishing boats in the harbour at Sesimbra

Palácio de Queluz ❾

In 1747, Pedro, son of João V, commissioned the architect Mateus Vicente to transform his 17th-century hunting lodge into a Rococo summer palace. After his marriage in 1760 to the future Maria I, the palace was again extended. The French architect Jean-Baptiste Robillion added the pavilion and gardens, made space for the Throne Room and redesigned the Music Room.

The bright Corredor das Mangas *(Corridor of Sleeves) is lined with 18th-century* azulejos *panels.*

The Don Quixote Chamber *is the royal bedroom where Pedro IV was born and died.*

Shell
Waterfall

The Sala dos Embaixadores, *built by Robillion, was used for diplomatic audiences as well as concerts. The trompe l'oeil ceiling shows the royal family attending a concert.*

The Music Room was the venue for operas and concerts performed by Maria I's talented orchestra.

The elegant Throne Room was the scene of splendid balls and banquets. The gilded statues of Atlas are by Silvestre Faria Lobo.

Chapel

Entrance

Malta Gardens

The Hanging Gardens, designed by Robillion, were built over arches, raising the ground in front of the palace.

VISITORS' CHECKLIST

14 km (9 miles) NW of Lisbon. Tel 214 343 860. **Palace and Gardens** Open 9am–5pm Wed–Mon (gardens to 6pm May–Oct). Adm charge.

The formal palace gardens, adorned with statues, fountains and topiary, were often used for entertaining.

The beautiful coastal scenery of the Serra da Arrábida

Serra da Arrábida ⑬

34 km (21 miles) SE of Lisbon.

The Parque Natural da Arrábida covers the small range of mountains that stretches along the coast between Sesimbra and Setúbal. It was established to protect the beautiful scenery and rich variety of birds and wildlife. The south-facing slopes are covered with aromatic shrubs and trees. Vineyards also thrive on the slopes and the town of Vila Nogueira de Azeitão is known for its wine.

The Estrada de Escarpa snakes along the ridge and affords astounding views. Just east of Sesimbra, the Serra da Arrábida drops to the sea in the sheer 380-m (1,250-ft) cliffs of Risco, the highest in mainland Portugal.

Convento da Arrábida

Serra da Arrábida. Open 3pm Wed–Sun (by appt only). Closed Aug. Adm charge.

Half-hidden by the trees of the Serra, this 16th-century building was formerly a Franciscan monastery. It now houses a cultural centre.

Museu Oceanográfico

Fortaleza de Santa Maria, Portinho da Arrábida. Open Tue–Sat. Adm charge.

This small fort now houses a Sea Museum and Marine Biology Centre where visitors can see aquaria filled with local sea creatures.

José Maria da Fonseca

Vila Nogueira de Azeitao. Open Sun–Fri. Adm charge.

This winery produces quality table wines and is famous for its fragrant dessert wine, Moscatel de Setúbal. Tours are available.

Palmela ⑭

41 km (25 miles) SE of Lisbon.

The formidable castle at Palmela stands over the small hill town, high on a northeastern spur of the wooded Serra da Arrábida. Its strategic position dominates the plain for miles around. In 1423, the castle became a monastery, which has now been converted into a hotel. From the castle terraces, there are fantastic views all around. The annual wine festival is held on the first weekend of September in front of the town hall.

The castle at Palmela with views over the Serra da Arrábida

One of Setúbal's architectural treasures – the Igreja de Jesus

Setúbal ⓰

48 km (30 miles) SE of Lisbon.

Although this is an important industrial town, Setúbal is a good base from which to explore the area. To the south is the harbour area and covered market. To the north is the old town, with its pedestrianized streets. The 16th-century cathedral has glorious tiled panels and gilded altar decoration.

Igreja de Jesus

Largo de Jesus. Open Tue–Sun.
Museum Open Tue–Sat.

This Gothic church was designed by the architect Diogo Boitac in 1494. In the old monastic quarters, a small museum houses 14 paintings of the life of Christ.

Museu de Arqueologia e Etnografia

Avenida Luísa Todi 162.
Open Tue–Sat.

The archaeological museum displays a wealth of finds from digs around Setúbal. The ethnography display shows local arts, crafts and industries, including the processing of salt and cork over the centuries.

Castelo de São Filipe

Estrada de São Filipe. Open daily.

This fort was built in 1595 by Philip II of Spain to keep an eye on pirates, invaders and locals. The interior now houses a hotel and a small chapel. A broad terrace offers views over the city and the Sado estuary.

Península de Tróia ⓰

136 km (84 miles) SE of Lisbon.

High-rise holiday apartments dominate the tip of the Tróia Peninsula, but from here stretch 18 km (11 miles) of untouched sandy beaches. Near Tróia, in the sheltered lagoon, the Roman town of Cetóbriga was the site of a thriving fish-salting business. To the south, holiday villas and golf clubs are springing up along the lagoon. Further on, Carrasqueira is an old fishing community and from here to Alcácer do Sal, pine forests line the road.

Alcácer do Sal ⓱

92 km (57 miles) SE of Lisbon.

The ancient town of Alcácer do Sal sits peacefully on the north bank of the River Sado. The castle was a hillfort as early as the 6th century BC and was claimed by the Phoenicians, Romans and Moors before being conquered by Afonso II in 1217. The buildings have now taken on a new life as a hotel. There are cafés along the riverside promenade and several historic churches.

Getting Around

One of the best ways to explore this attractive city is on foot. However, it's a hilly place, and public transport is a good alternative for the way-weary. Lisbon has an extensive network of trams, lifts, funiculars and buses, and a metro system. Driving around this congested city is not recommended.

On Foot

Walking is a great way to take in the sights, especially in the old neighbourhoods of the Alfama and the Bairro Alto. There are walking tours, such as the day trips organized by Inside Tours (www.insidelisbon.com).

Funiculars and Lifts

Due to Lisbon's hills, funiculars (elevadors) and lifts are a good way of getting from river level to the upper parts of the city. They also afford some superb views.

Metro sign

Buses

Lisbon buses (autocarros) are usually yellow with a few orange ones and they go just about anywhere. Most inner-city services run from 5:30am to 1am. A smaller number of night buses run from 1am to 5:30am. Tickets can be bought on boarding.

Trams

Trams (eléctricos) only operate in a very limited area of the city, along the river to Belém and around the hilly parts of Lisbon.

Single tickets for all rides are very cheap except for those on the red *Colinas* or *Tejo* trams. These offer special sightseeing trips around Lisbon for tourists.

The Metro

The best way to get around town is via the Metro, called the *Metropolitano*. Metro stations are sign-posted with a red M and the service operates from 6:30am to 1am each day. The system is safe to travel on even at night, and trains run frequently. There are 46 stations operating on four lines. These lines link the Metro to major bus, train and ferry services, and provide transport from Lisbon's suburbs to the heart of the city.

Buying Tickets

Buses, trams and funiculars all use the same ticket, which can be bought on boarding, but it is cheaper to buy tickets in advance. You can get these from Carris kiosks in many parts of the city. Metro tickets are bought in machines or from ticket offices at the stations. The Lisboa card is a special tourist pass that allows free access to most forms of public transport. It is on sale at the airport, some hotels and sights, tourist offices and Carris kiosks.

Taxis

Taxis in Portugal remain relatively cheap. Most taxis are beige but a few of the older black and green cabs still exist. All are metered, although costs depend on the time of day. Taxis can be hailed on the street or ordered by phone.

Driving

Most car hire companies have offices at the airport. Driving around Lisbon is not advisable but if you have to, avoid the rush hours and carry your car insurance, passport, licence, and rental contract with you.

Travelling around Lisbon and the Coast

Lisbon and its surroundings offer numerous sightseeing opportunities and the good road network means that most sights are only 30 minutes or so from the city centre. Buses, coaches and local trains are available for visiting Cascais and Estoril. Although no public buses go to Sintra, there are organized coach tours to the palaces and the glorious countryside around the town. Tours can be booked through a travel agent, with a tour operator or at some hotels. A frequent rail service operates from Rossio station in Lisbon to Sintra. To visit Sesimbra and other areas south of the Tagus, ferries depart from Praça do Comércio. Alternatively, the Fertagus train crosses the Ponte 25 de Abril bridge on a lower level. Trains and buses can then be picked up on the south bank of the Tagus.

Façade of Rossio Station, which operates trains to Sintra

TRAVEL INFORMATION

TRAINS

Carminos de Ferro Portugueses (CP)
(state-owned railway)
Tel 808 208 208.

COACHES

EVA
Tel 213 581 466.
Rede Expressos
Tel 213 577 915.

CAR RENTAL

Avis Tel 218 435 550.
Budget Tel 218 495 523.
Hertz Tel 219 426 300.

24-HOUR TAXIS

Autocoope Tel 217 932 756.
Teletáxis Tel 218 111 100.
Retalis Rádio Táxis Tel 218 119 000.

Survival Guide

Lisbon has become increasingly cosmopolitan over the past decade, and is better-equipped than ever to receive visitors. This section includes information on money, telephones, Internet access, the postal service and what to do in an emergency.

Public pay phone

MONEY

Currency

Portugal uses the common European currency of euros and cents. There are 100 cents to a euro. Notes come in €5, €10, €20, €50 and €100 denominations. Coins come in 1c, 2c, 5c, 10c, 20c, 50c, €1 and €2 pieces.

Banking and Exchange Facilities

Money can be changed at banks, bureaux de change *(agências de câmbios)* and at many hotels. Bank branches are everywhere, but their rates of exchange and commissions vary. They are open between 8:30am and 3pm, Monday to Friday.

Traveller's Cheques and Credit Cards

Traveller's cheques are the safest way to carry money, but cashing them can be quite expensive in Lisbon, and they are rarely taken as payment. Credit and debit cards are a more convenient option. Automatic teller machines (Multibanco or MB) are typically found outside bank branches or in shopping centres. Most machines accept Visa, MasterCard, American Express, Maestro and Cirrus.

COMMUNICATIONS

Telephones

Public pay phones come in both the coin and the card variety, as well as in combinations of the two. They are found in booths in the street as well as in bars, cafés and shopping centres. Phone cards are available from post offices, newsagents, tobacconists and Telecom company outlets. To call Portugal, use the country code 351. To call abroad from Lisbon, dial 00 and then the country code. Lisbon's directory enquiries number is 118 and for international directory enquiries dial 177.

Internet Access

Internet cafés are found in various places around the city, including two of the three main shopping centres, Columbo and Monumental. Most internet cafés also have WiFi access, as do most hotels, post offices, petrol stations as well as the airport.

Postal Service

Correios (post offices) are dotted around the city, but for buying stamps use the red, coin-operated dispensers as this will save you joining long queues. First-class mail is called *correio azul*. The main post office on Restauradores is open at weekends; others operate 9am to 6pm weekdays.

HEALTH & SAFETY

Police

In Lisbon and other main towns, the police force is the *Polícia de Segurança Pública* (PSP). In rural areas, law and order is maintained by the *Guarda Nacional Republicana* (GNR). The *Brigada de Trânsito* (traffic police) are a division of the GNR, and are recognizable by their red armbands. They are responsible for patrolling roads.

Emergencies

The number to contact in the event of an emergency is 112. Dial the number and then indicate which service you require – the police *(polícia)*, an ambulance *(ambulância)* or the fire brigade *(bombeiros)*. If you need medical treatment, the casualty department *(serviço de urgência)* of the closest main hospital will treat you. The British Hospital in Lisbon has

A yellow Lisbon ambulance

English-speaking doctors, as do international health centres on the Lisbon Coast.

Pharmacies

Pharmacies *(farmácias)* in Lisbon can diagnose simple health problems. Pharmacists can dispense a range of drugs that would normally only be available on prescription in many other countries. The sign for a *farmácia* is a green cross. They are open from 9am to 1pm and 3pm to 7pm (9am to 1pm Saturdays).

Pharmacy sign

Personal Safety

Violent crime is fairly rare in Portugal. However, you should try to avoid quiet areas such as the Baixa after dark, and don't stroll alone through Bairro Alto, Alfama or around Cais do Sodré after the bars have closed for the night.

DIRECTORY

General Emergency
(Fire, Police, Ambulance)
Tel 112.

British Hospital
Tel 213 943 100.

AP Portugal
(offers language services, such as interpreting)
Tel 213 303 759.

Ordem dos Advogados
(lawyers' association)
Tel 218 875 621.

Index

Acknowledgments

Dorling Kindersley would like to thank the following people whose help and assistance contributed to the preparation of this book.

Design and Editorial
Publisher Douglas Amrine
List Manager Julie Oughton
Design Manager Mabel Chan
Editor Alexandra Whittleton
Project Editor Andrea Pinnington
Project Designer Sunita Gahir
Fact-Checker Mark Harding
Picture Research Ellen Root
Cartography Stuart James
Production Controller Imogen Boase
DTP Designer Jason Little
Jacket Designer Tracy Smith

Additional Photography
Rough Guides/Eddie Gerald;
Tony Souter; Peter Wilson

Picture Credits
Every effort has been made to trace the copyright holders of images, and we apologize in advance for any unintentional omissions. We would be pleased to insert the appropriate acknowledgments in any subsequent edition of this publication.

Picture Key
t = top; tl = top left; tc = top centre; tr = top right; cla = centre left above; ca = centre above; cra = centre right above; cl = centre left; c = centre; cr = centre right; clb = centre left below; cb = centre below; crb = centre right below; bl = bottom left; b = bottom; bc = bottom centre; br = bottom right.

The Publishers would like to thank the following individuals, companies and picture libraries for their kind permission to reproduce their photographs:

ALAMY IMAGES: Peter Horree 76tl; Melvyn Longhurst 46; Richard Wareham Fotografie 14t; David Soulsby 75bl; Ken Welsh 41tl. CALOUSTE GULBENKIAN MUSEUM, LISBON: 50b, 50t, 51t. ©MUSEU NACIONAL DE ARTE ANTIGA, LISBOA; INSTITUTO DOS MUSEUS E DA CONSERVAÇÃO – MC: 32bl, 32cr, 33c. PALACIO DA PENA: 66cla. PHOTOLIBRARY: age fotostock/Kordcom Kordcom 56.

JACKET
Front – ALAMY IMAGES: Art Kowalsky t. Back – DORLING KINDERSLEY: Rough Guides/Eddie Gerald t.

All other images © DORLING KINDERSLEY

For further information see www.dkimages.com

Price Codes are for a three-course meal per person including tax, service and half a bottle of house wine.
Cheap under €30
Moderate €30–50
Expensive €50 or more

SPECIAL EDITIONS OF DK TRAVEL GUIDES

Phrase Book

In Emergency

Help!	**Socorro!**	soo-koh-roo
Stop!	**Páre!**	pahr'
Call a doctor!	**Chame um médico!**	shahm' ooñ meh-dee-koo
Call an ambulance!	**Chame uma ambulância!**	shahm' oo-muh añ-boo-lañ-see-uh
Call the police!	**Chame a polícia!**	shahm'uh poo-lee-see-uh
Call the fire brigade!	**Chame os bombeiros!**	shahm' oosh bom-bay-roosh
Where is the nearest telephone?	**Há um telefone aqui perto?**	ah ooñ te-le-fon' uh-keepehr-too
Where is the nearest hospital?	**Onde é o hospital mais próximo?**	ond' eh oo ohsh-pee-tahl' mysh pro-see-moo

Communication Essentials

Yes	**Sim**	seeñ
No	**Não**	nowñ
Please	**Por favor/ Faz favor**	poor fuh-vor fash fuh-vor
Thank you	**Obrigado/da**	o-bree-gah-doo/duh
Excuse me	**Desculpe**	dish-koolp'
Hello	**Olá**	oh-lah
Goodbye	**Adeus**	a-deh-oosh
Here	**Aqui**	uh-kee
What?	**O quê?**	oo keh
Why?	**Porquê?**	poor-keh
Where?	**Onde?**	oñd'

Useful Phrases

How are you?	**Como está?**	koh-moo shtah
Very well, thank you.	**Bem, obrigado/da.**	bayñ o-bree-gah-doo/duh
Where is/are … ?	**Onde está/estão … ?**	ond' shtah/ shtowñ
How far is it to … ?	**A que distância fica … ?**	uh kee dish-tañ-see-uh fee-kuh
Do you speak English?	**Fala inglês?**	fah-luh eeñ-glehsh
I don't understand.	**Não compreendo.**	nowñ kom-pree-eñ-doo
Could you speak more slowly please?	**Pode falar mais devagar por favor?**	pohd' fuh-lar mysh d'-va-gar poor fuh-vor
I'm sorry.	**Desculpe.**	dish-koolp'

Useful Words

Big	**grande**	grañd'
Small	**pequeno**	pe-keh-noo
Hot	**quente**	keñt'
Cold	**frio**	free-oo
Good	**bom**	boñ
Bad	**mau**	mah-oo
Quite a lot/enough	**bastante**	bash-tañt'
Open	**aberto**	a-behr-too
Closed	**fechado**	fe-shah-doo
Left	**esquerda**	shkehr-duh
Right	**direita**	dee-ray-tuh